# WHEN A CHILD WANDERS

# ♔

## ROBERT L. MILLET

Deseret Book Company
Salt Lake City, Utah

ISBN 1-57345-142-8

Printed in the United States of America

10   9   8   7   6   5   4   3   2   1

# WHEN A CHILD WANDERS

*Who are these straying sheep—*

*these wayward sons and daughters?*

*They are children of the Covenant,*

*heirs to the promises,*

*and have received, if baptized,*

*the gift of the Holy Ghost,*

*which makes manifest the things of God.*

*Could all that go for naught?*

ORSON F. WHITNEY

# CONTENTS

# PREFACE

It is a glorious thing to observe young people as they begin to respond to the promptings of the Spirit, grow in spiritual graces, and become productive and contributing members of the kingdom of God on earth. Nothing brings more satisfaction to parents or loved ones than watching the youth of the Church become all that they were meant to become. But tragically, some of the rising generation do not reach for the rod of iron, do not follow the examples of parents or Church leaders, do not acquire the conviction or develop the commitment to the Church that we had anticipated. Some children drift aimlessly, remaining only a stone's throw away from full activity; others vigorously turn away from time-honored values and embrace the ways of a degenerate world.

This work focuses on the phenomenon of wandering

children. It is not meant to make us all feel a little better in knowing that others share our pain. It is, rather, a call for us to have hope—hope for the future, hope for those who now seem so hopeless, hope for reconciliation and reunion. Such hope is not based on the power of positive thinking, though it is good to be positive; it is, rather, based on doctrine—sound, solid doctrine—doctrine from the prophets that offers us true and lasting hope for the future in the face of present ills and challenges with our children or other loved ones.

So much of our hopelessness stems from our inability to comprehend and thus lay hold on the grand prophetic promises that await those who are true and faithful to their covenants. In so many matters that matter, Joseph Smith the Seer has opened celestial windows and beckoned the Saints of the Most High to gaze with him upon the scenes of eternity. He has called upon us to repent of small-mindedness and broaden our horizons. As a supernal comfort to those whose children wander for a season, he implores us to search the scriptures, ponder the revelations of God's covenant spokesmen, and believe the soothing word regarding the power of the gospel covenant. This book seeks to point us toward those consummate blessings that can be ours if we trust in and rely upon the Lord Jesus, the Mediator of the Covenant. It is an invitation for us to focus on things that matter most—covenants, ordinances, families, sealing power, and righteousness. That all who read these pages may feel to glory in the power of the gospel and thereby rejoice in "the testimony of the covenant" (D&C 109:38), is my sincere prayer.

In the preparation of this work, I am deeply indebted to many who offered counsel, consolation, and references, as well as others who helped to sharpen my focus on this singularly significant doctrinal theme. It is always a bit awkward to mention specific people, but I express particular thanks to my colleagues Larry E. Dahl, Leon R. Hartshorn, E. Dale LeBaron, Robert J. Matthews, Joseph F. McConkie, Keith W. Perkins, Rex C. Reeve Jr., Stephen E. Robinson, M. Catherine Thomas, and Brent L. Top. I am indebted to Lori Soza, a dedicated and competent secretary and assistant, for her knowledgeable assistance in preparing the manuscript for publication. I acknowledge also the encouragement of Sheri Dew of Deseret Book Company and especially the keen and caring editorial eye of Suzanne Brady; Suzanne has simply made this a better book. Though I am indebted to so many for so much, I alone am responsible for the conclusions drawn from the evidence cited. This book is a private endeavor and thus not an official publication of either The Church of Jesus Christ of Latter-day Saints or Brigham Young University.

# PROLOGUE

Most of us enter upon family life with grand expectations and high hopes. We feel secure that if we simply do our jobs properly—attend church, study the scriptures and pray as individuals and families, hold family home evenings, pay our tithing, love and serve one another and those within our community—happiness and joy will flow into our lives. We teach our children the principles of the gospel, kneel in prayer with them, participate in mother-daughter activities and Pinewood Derbies, and feel confident that in the end we will enjoy the fruits of our labors—that each little boy and each little girl will grow up with the same depth of testimony and the same level of commitment to God and the restored gospel that we as parents or loved ones have.

Most of us anticipate that our little ones will grow up to be faithful and participating Latter-day Saints. We believe that our children will be involved in all of the programs of the Church—Young Women recognition, Eagle Scout awards, seminary graduation, institute of religion enrollment, and so on. When things do not materialize as we had planned and when some of our long-held goals for the children are definitely not being achieved or even pursued, the stark realities of life set in. Life doesn't always turn out exactly as we had planned.

The phenomenon of wandering children and the trail of attendant sorrows are no respecter of persons. They make their way into the homes of rich and poor, active and less active, functional and dysfunctional. They raise their ugly heads in families led by single parents as well as in families presided over by bishops and stake presidents. They take their toll on abusive and negligent mothers and fathers as well as on mothers and fathers of faith, people who are sincerely trying to do what's right.

Many Latter-day Saint families have become intimately acquainted with heartache and suffering and agony and a roller coaster of emotions. They have felt the despair that comes from seeing loved ones violate their covenants, turn away from what they have been taught, and despise what they once loved. Parents cringe as they watch their precious young people close doors of opportunity to themselves through foolish choices. Many mothers and fathers come to know some things quite well—what it means to pour out their souls to God in prayer in behalf of loved ones; how to fast with real intent; the inestimable value of attending the temple in a search for solace; how to love when it seems so natural to hate, to be firm when it would be so much easier to crumble; and how to face each day and keep going through the divine grace or enabling power that the Great Physician promises to those who mourn.

I confess that I do not have the solutions to such vexing problems, but I have wrestled intensely with the questions. I know what it feels like to be haunted by feelings of inadequacy in dealing with my children, to browbeat myself for not being more faithful as a parent on this or that issue, to wonder at weak moments if it's all worth it. I assure you that I would much rather have learned some of the harsh lessons of family life by reading of the experience of others. But there are some things we cannot go around; we

must go through. And through it all, through the
tears and the toil and the torturous interrogation
of the heart, there comes the quiet assurance that
the God of heaven knows and cares. He knows
perfectly. He cares deeply and profoundly.

Through it all, there comes also a compassion and an empathy for others who mourn. We
find ourselves much less prone to judge, much
less eager to place blame and assign guilt—
largely because we have become more closely
acquainted with the hurt of the hurting.
Through the process of trying to understand
how to act, how not to act, how to feel, how not
to feel, what to say, what not to say—through
it all, we find comfort and direction from the
Holy Spirit and from the scriptures and the
words of living oracles. We find principles—
doctrinal and practical—that give us hope, provide perspective, and prompt patience. This
book deals with some of those principles.

This work is not a collection of child-rearing
techniques, a behavior modification manual, or
a guide on how to communicate with children.
Rather, it is an effort to set forth a theological

foundation for hope in family living, especially
when our families fall short of the high standard
we and the Lord have set for us. More specifi-
cally, matters to be discussed include

• the power that comes from focusing on
fundamentals;

• the challenge of moral agency and the
unique pain associated with straying children;

• the nature, transforming power, and supernal benefits of life within the covenant;

• the power of the gospel covenant to bind
and seal on earth and in heaven; and

• the power of that covenant to reach out to
wandering sheep and restore them to the fold.

One word is central to all that is discussed in
this book. That word is *power.* The gospel of
Jesus Christ is "the power of God unto salvation"
(Romans 1:16). There is power in the person of
Jesus Christ, consummate power in his gospel,
inexpressible power in the covenant we make
with him through membership in his church
and kingdom. Because the family is the central
unit in God's eternal plan for the salvation of his
children, Satan will draw upon all of the

weapons in his insidious arsenal to discredit, dismiss, and dismantle the family. But God is the supreme governor of the universe. He holds all things in his power. At his word and by virtue of his power, we are created, renewed, and redeemed. I have come to know that he will preserve us as members of his royal family if we trust in him and rely upon the merits and mercy and grace of the Holy Messiah. The sheep of his fold may wander for a season, but if we hope on, pray on, and trust in the prophetic promises, the Mediator of the Covenant will work mighty miracles and thereby accomplish his "strange act" through us (D&C 95:4). Of that eternal verity we may rest assured. "Keep all the commandments and covenants by which ye are bound; and I will cause the heavens to shake for your good, and Satan shall tremble and Zion shall rejoice upon the hills and flourish; and Israel shall be saved in mine own due time; and by the keys which I have given shall they be led, and no more be confounded at all" (D&C 35:24–25).

# FIRST THINGS FIRST

I t is so very easy in today's busy and complex world to get caught up in the thick of thin things, to become prey to the less important. Programs and procedures begin to take priority over people. Means begin to occupy us more than ends. Making a living, being included in the best social circles, providing the family with nice cars, lovely clothes, or extravagant travel opportunities—these may make life enjoyable and comfortable, but they are not the stuff of which eternal happiness is made. Life is a mission, not a career. We come here to gain experience and to acquire the attributes of godliness. At least as important as knowledge and experience and spiritual growth are relationships. We have been sent to earth to learn to live together in love, to build and perpetuate the family. Indeed, the family is one of the few things that will continue into the eternities.

## A Plan of Happiness

It is marvelous beyond expression to know that there is meaning to some of life's madness, that there is purpose to it all. That God our

Father does indeed have a plan, a program for
the development, growth, and happiness of his
children is soothing to the soul. There are times
when I simply could not go on if I did not
know in my heart that the Almighty is aware of
us, aware of our challenges, our pain, and our
doubts. "Search diligently, pray always, and be
believing," the Savior counsels us in a modern
revelation, "and all things shall work together for
your good, if ye walk uprightly and remember
the covenant wherewith ye have covenanted
one with another" (D&C 90:24). Latter-day Saints
know from scripture, through living oracles, and
by the still, small voice that we lived before we
came here; that we are here not by chance but
as a part of a grand and divinely orchestrated
plan; and that when our time on earth is finished, we will continue to expand and improve
in another sphere. In short, life is eternal. It is
meant to be enjoyable and rewarding, but it is
also to be lived soberly and godly, because eternal consequences hang in the balance.

People matter more than things. People
matter more than schedules and timetables and

products. God and Christ work full time in the business of people, and perhaps that primary labor contributes measurably to their fulness of joy. Sometimes when the most important things get crowded out by the least important, the Lord finds a way to jerk us back to reality and focus us on fundamentals. Occasionally that reality check comes through a staggering confrontation with death, the stark realization that we are here on earth for only a brief season. Often it comes through what we call tragedy—an injury, a crippling disease, a severe trauma. And once in a while it comes through incidents much less dramatic but equally direct. What does it profit us if we gain the whole world and then, because of neglect or distraction, forfeit the eternal associations that bring the deepest feelings of fulfillment?

Many years ago I sat on the floor in front of a small bookcase in the dining room of our tiny two-bedroom apartment. I was immersed in reading and referencing and marking; deadlines were crowding in on me. Ironically, I was perusing President David O. McKay's book *Gospel Ideals* when Angela, my two-and-a-half-year-old daughter, walked over to me and asked me to join her, her one-year-old brother, David, and their mother in some games they were playing on the floor a few feet away. I responded to Angie that I was very busy and couldn't make it. Within three minutes David crawled over and asked: "Dad, you come play?" I called out to my wife at that point: "Shauna, can't you see that what I am doing is important? Could you please keep these children out of my hair until I finish this project?"

I dived back into my research. But then I felt my attention being drawn back to the threesome, almost as if I were being turned about physically. I looked into three pairs of eyes and what I saw was very unsettling—there was hurt and, in Shauna's eyes, at least, a bit of frustration. A voice came into my mind. Whether it was the voice of the Holy Ghost or the voice of conscience, I don't know: it was nevertheless an inner awareness of my duty. It stated simply but boldly: "Brother, behold the plan of salvation!" In that brief instant there came an avalanche of feelings—feelings of perspective, for in a flash I saw and felt things as they really were; feelings of overwhelming love for a trusting wife and adoring children; and yes, feelings of guilt for neglecting the most important people in my life. A rapidly repentant father crawled over to his family and became involved in things that really matter.

In the years since that experience, I have reflected again and again on what I felt that evening. Maybe it was a consuming love for my family, combined with a cold slap in the face, that awakened me momentarily. Other things over the years have served a similar function. Shauna has gotten my attention occasionally when I have chosen to bury myself in a book and ignore the family. She has said simply: "Bob, if you're not careful, you may grow up to be a very intelligent ministering angel." That works, too. I haven't always been the greatest husband and father since that red-letter day in my life, but I have been better. And it is amazing how we can be tutored by the medium of memory.

## Our Best for Our Loved Ones

One really ironic thing I have noticed is our frequent unwillingness to be as patient and forgiving with family members as we are with friends, associates, or even strangers. Most of us wouldn't consider publicly insulting a colleague or belittling an acquaintance or slipping into the silent treatment with co-workers at church. But we often do such things to those who matter most to us. Because we desperately want our little ones to be ever so much better than we were, we tend to become impatient with their lack of progress, irritated at their mistakes in judgment, and downright angry about their failings. I have far too often caught myself shaking my head and wondering when the spirit of life and good judgment would descend upon my teenagers, especially when their choices were not as wise as I would have preferred. If the Lord had wanted to put a forty-year-old head on the shoulders of a sixteen-year-old, I suppose he would have done so; instead, he almost always attaches the head (and heart and emotions and hormones) of a sixteen-year-old to a sixteen-year-old.

Jeffrey R. Holland once described a similar painful situation in his own family: "Early in our married life my young family and I were laboring through graduate school at a university in New England. Pat was the Relief Society president in our ward, and I was serving in our stake presidency. I was going to school full-time and teaching half-time. We had two small children then, with little money and lots of pressures.

"One evening I came home from long hours at school, feeling the proverbial weight of the world on my shoulders. Everything seemed to be especially demanding and discouraging and dark. I wondered if the dawn would ever come. Then, as I walked into our small student apartment, there was an unusual silence in the room.

"'What's the trouble?' I asked.

"'Matthew has something he wants to tell you,' Pat said.

"'Matt, what do you have to tell me?' He was quietly playing with his toys in the corner of the room, trying very hard not to hear me. 'Matt,' I said a little louder, 'do you have something to tell me?'

"He stopped playing, but for a moment he didn't look up. Then two enormous, tear-filled brown eyes turned toward me, and with the pain only a five-year-old can know, he said, 'I didn't mind Mommy tonight, and I spoke back to her.' With that he burst into tears, and his entire little body shook with grief. A childish indiscretion had been noted, a painful confession had been offered, the growth of a five-year-old was continuing, and loving reconciliation could have been wonderfully underway.

"Everything might have been just terrific—except for me. If you can imagine such an idiotic thing, I lost my temper. It wasn't that I lost it with Matt—it was with a hundred and one other things on my mind. But he didn't know that, and I wasn't disciplined enough to admit it. He got the whole load of bricks.

"I told him how disappointed I was and how much more I thought I could have expected from him. I sounded like the parental pygmy I was. Then I did what I had never done before in his life: I told him that he was to go straight to bed and that I would not be in to say his prayers with him or to tell him a bedtime story. Muffling his sobs, he obediently went to his bedside, where he knelt—alone—to say his prayers. Then he stained his little pillow with tears his father should have been wiping away.

"If you think the silence upon my arrival was heavy, you should have felt it now. Pat did not say a word. She didn't have to. I felt terrible!

"Later, as we knelt by our own bed, my feeble prayer for blessings upon my family fell back on my ears with a horrible, hollow ring. I wanted to get up off my knees right then and go to Matt and ask his forgiveness, but he was long since peacefully asleep.

"My own relief was not so soon coming, but finally I fell asleep and began to dream, which I seldom do. I dreamed Matt and I were packing two cars for a move. For some reason his mother and baby sister were not present. As we finished I turned to him and said, 'Okay, Matt, you drive one car and I'll drive the other.'

"This five-year-old very obediently crawled up on the seat and tried to grasp the massive steering wheel. I walked over to the other car and started the motor. As I began to pull away, I looked to see how my son was doing. He was trying—oh, how he was trying. He tried to reach the pedals, but he couldn't. He was also turning knobs and pushing buttons, trying to start the motor. He could scarcely be seen over the dashboard, but there staring out at me again were those same immense, tear-filled, beautiful brown eyes. As I pulled away, he cried out, 'Daddy, don't leave me. I don't know how to do it. I'm too little.' And I drove away.

"A short time later, driving down that desert road in my dream, I suddenly realized in one stark, horrifying moment what I had done. I slammed my car to a stop, threw open the door, and started to run as fast as I could. I left car, keys, belongings, and all—and I ran. The pavement was so hot it burned my feet, and tears blinded my straining effort to see this child somewhere on the horizon. I kept running, praying, pleading to be forgiven and to find my boy safe and secure.

"As I rounded a curve, nearly ready to drop from physical and emotional exhaustion, I saw the unfamiliar car I had left Matt to drive. It was pulled carefully off to the side of the road, and he was laughing and playing nearby. An older man was with him, playing and responding to his games. Matt saw me and cried out something like, 'Hi, Dad. We're having fun.' Obviously he had already forgiven and forgotten my terrible transgression against him.

"But I dreaded the older man's gaze, which followed my every move. I tried to say 'Thank you,' but his eyes were filled with sorrow and disappointment. I muttered an awkward apology and the stranger said simply, 'You should not have left him alone to do this difficult thing. It would not have been asked of you.'

"With that, the dream ended, and I shot upright in bed. My pillow was stained, whether with perspiration or tears I do not know. I threw off the covers and ran to the little metal camp cot that was my son's bed. There on my knees and through my tears I cradled him in my arms and spoke to him while he slept. I told him that every dad makes mistakes but that they don't mean to. I told him it wasn't his fault I had had a bad day. I told him that when boys are five or fifteen, dads sometimes forget and think they are fifty. I told him that I wanted him to be a small boy for a long, long time, because all too soon he would grow up and be a man and wouldn't be playing on the floor with his toys when I came home. I told him that I loved him and his mother and his sister more than anything in the world, and that whatever challenges we had in life, we would face them together. I told him that never again would I withhold my affection or my forgiveness from him, and never, I prayed, would he withhold them from me. I told him I was honored to be his father and that I would try with all my heart to be worthy of such a great responsibility" (*On Earth As It Is in Heaven*, 165–68).

Many years ago Boyd K. Packer spoke to the youth: "Some day—some day soon for some of you—you are going to have the marvelous experience of learning to love someone else more than you love yourself. This is a crowning achievement in life, yet countless thousands live out there in this world and do not achieve this experience. It does not come, I think, in a courtship or even on a honeymoon; but it is a reward for building this little [family] kingdom. Someday when you hold a little boy or a little girl in your arms and know that he or she belongs to you, this experience may come to you.

"I recall on one occasion, when I was returning from seminary to my home for lunch, that as I drove in, my wife met me in the driveway. I could tell by the expression on her face that something was wrong. 'Cliff has been killed,' she said. 'They want you to come over.' As I hastened around the corner to where Cliff lived with his wife and four sons and his little daughter, I saw Cliff lying in the middle of the highway with a blanket over him. The ambulance was just pulling away with little Colleen. Cliff had been on his way out to the farm and had stopped to cross the street to take little Colleen to her mother who waited on the opposite curb. But the child, as children will, broke from her father's hand and slipped into the street. A large truck was coming. Cliff jumped from the curb and pushed his little daughter from the path of the truck—but he wasn't soon enough.

"A few days later I had the responsibility of talking at the funeral of Cliff and little Colleen. Someone said, 'What a terrible waste. Certainly he ought to have stayed on the curb. He knew the child might have died. But he had four sons and a wife to provide for. What a pathetic waste!' And I estimated that that individual never had had the experience of loving someone more than he loved himself.

"To you who are young, this experience of loving someone more than you love yourself can come, insofar as I know, only through the exercise of the power of creation. Through it you become really Christian, and you know, as few others know, what the word 'Father' means when it is spoken of in the scriptures; and you feel some of the love and concern that He has for us, and you may experience some of the remorse and sorrow that must be His if we fail to accept all that is beautiful and praiseworthy and of good report in this world" (*Problems in Teaching the Moral Standard,* 10–11).

I have come to know of the truthfulness and import of those words. There are family joys that transcend anything earthly, just as there are family sorrows that tear at the heart and wound the emotions in ways impossible to describe.

These feelings, highs and lows, come only to those who love their children more than they love themselves. I would have been tempted to ask that the agony of the lows be removed if I had not comprehended the majesty and supernal joy of the highs. When I have watched helplessly as my little ones experienced deep sorrow or chose foolishly, I have yearned to take their place, take their part, take their pain. I have remembered Moses, who went into the holy mountain to receive God's law. While he was gone, the children of Israel molded a golden calf and gave themselves up to gross wickedness. Moses broke the first set of tablets that contained the higher law and put the idolaters to death. "And Moses returned unto the Lord, and said, Oh, this people have sinned a great sin, and have made them gods of gold. Yet now, if thou wilt forgive their sin—; and if not, blot me, I pray thee, out of thy book which thou hast written" (Exodus 32:31–32). I have learned to feel with Moses his mediational plea: heaven would surely not be heaven without those I love.

Several years ago I knelt beside my father

during the closing hours of his life. My dad was a large man and was active, involved, and the life of any social gathering for as long as I could remember. I still recall watching him lead the fast breaks in basketball (he played in a city league and in Church tournaments during those years). I now looked upon a body that had become emaciated and ravaged by mortality, one that was appropriately eager to be laid to rest. As Dad napped for a few moments during those closing hours, I thought of his success in business and of how much he was respected in the community. I thought of his leadership in the Church. He had been my bishop, had sent me on a mission, and then had served for many years in the stake presidency. He had spoken at more funerals and had administered to the sick more often than most of us would do in three lifetimes. It was thus terribly difficult for the family to watch his body succumb to the pull of disease and death, to witness him lose his eyesight and then his strength.

On several occasions over the preceding years the two of us had discussed one of Dad's favorite subjects: the spirit world. Practically every time we got together he wanted to talk about life after death. This occasion was no different. He asked with a yearning in his voice: "Son, do you suppose my dad will meet me? I hope he does. It has been so long since I saw him." There was no fear of death, no dread of the unknown, and even some eagerness to acquire answers to questions he and I had debated for a long time. I thought of his accomplishments— of the friendships he had cultivated, the hundreds of people whose lives he had touched, the difference his life had made. I tried to comment on some of those things, but he would have none of it. He wanted to talk about his family and about my family. Family. Family. That was what he wanted to focus on. He pleaded with me to help Mom take care of my brothers and my sister. He spoke with me at some length about my wife, about how much he loved her, about how delighted he was that I had married her and how thrilled he was that I was so happy. He spoke of each of my children and asked me to convey to them how much their grandfather loved them and what great expectations he had for them.

Among the last things Dad did as I tucked him into bed that night was to pull me close to him and whisper, "Son, I haven't told you often enough how much I love you and how proud I am of you." I assured him that he had told me plenty of times and that there was never any doubt in my mind how he felt. He insisted, though, that I hear it again. We embraced tenderly for the last time. Then, as he lay holding onto time with one hand and eternity with the other, he let go of the former and clung to the latter.

Those moments are precious to me. They are a capstone to a mortal relationship as well as an invitation to renew that relationship when the Lord sees fit to call me to the next sphere. Again and again when I become preoccupied with things, when I am distracted by the ephemeral and the fleeting, I am reminded of what mattered most to Dad: his eternal family.

# WHEN A CHILD WANDERS

For Latter-day Saints who know what
matters most and what is and ought to be
at the top of our list of priorities, some
things hurt much more than others. It
hurts to bear our testimonies to friends and
loved ones who shun our witness as foolish and
absurd. It hurts to see the poverty and abuse
and neglect and degradation in society when we
know that the world's only hope is the gospel of
Jesus Christ. And it hurts when we do our best
to bring up our children in light and truth, only
to see some of them turn away from that light
and choose to walk in darkness. If the greatest
joys in life are family joys, then surely the greatest sorrows in life are family sorrows. If no other
success in life can compensate for failure in the
home, then what can be more painful than having wandering children? If the most important
work we will ever do in the Church is that
which we do within the walls of our own home,
then nothing causes deeper turmoil and
soul-searching than having children who stray
from the path of truth and righteousness.

Picture a priesthood leader introducing a

speaker in sacrament meeting: "We have asked Sister Johnson to speak on the importance of the family because of what a wonderful job she has done in her own family. As you know, all of her children graduated at the top of their high school classes and all have obtained college degrees." Or: "We have asked Brother Hastings to speak to us on the importance of preparing our children for missionary service. Brother Hastings must be doing something right, for all seven of his sons have served faithful missions." Now ponder what those people in the congregation feel whose children have dropped out of high school or have chosen not to serve missions. Yet we are a part of a Church that has very high ideals, and we must never lower the ideal. We take seriously the Master's commandment to be perfect, even though all of us fall short of such a standard. We speak of the importance of eternal marriage, even though some in the congregation may not have married in the temple. We preach of the vital nature of virtue and chastity, even though some in our midst may be in need of repentance. And we will forever hold up the family as the mainstay of society and the salvation of humankind, even though all human families fall short of the eternal ideal.

We have no choice but to declare what is and what should be. We do not lower our vision or dilute our ideals as a concession to a decaying society. And yet, there is much heartache among us, much distress over current failures in the home and family, even among the Latter-day Saints. The key is not to surrender our goals but to be more sensitive and solicitous of those who come up short. Not all of our little ones will be above average. Not all of our children will excel academically. Not all of our teenagers will be articulate, handsome, or charismatic. And not all of our posterity will choose the right. The odds are certainly greater that children will turn out properly if parents do their part to live the gospel, teach the gospel, and be active and involved in the Church. But we live in a world of risk; there are no guarantees. We knew that before we came here, and perhaps that is why so many of our spirit brothers and sisters followed Lucifer: "The contention in heaven was—Jesus said there would be certain souls that would not be saved; and the devil said he could save them all, and laid his plans before the grand council, who gave their vote in favor of Jesus Christ" (Smith, *Teachings of the Prophet Joseph Smith*, 357).

## The Joy and the Agony of Agency

I remember very well sitting in a high priests group meeting one Sunday morning. The instructor was delivering a lesson on the plan of salvation and focusing, for the moment, on agency. He had reminded us that there is no mention in scripture of free agency but rather of moral agency (see D&C 101:78). He bore his testimony of the centrality of agency, of how awful things would be if we were coerced to do good, and of how grateful we should be for this divinely bestowed gift. The instructor asked for others in the group to share their own testimonies and feelings of gratitude, which they did for about fifteen minutes. The mood was interrupted quite dramatically when one of the members of the group said, essentially: "Well, that's okay for you folks, and it's fine for me. I'm grateful that I have the right to choose. But to be honest, as far as my family is concerned, sometimes I wish there were no agency. Agency is painful, maybe the most painful thing I can think of. Brethren, I assure you that nothing hurts more than watching your children self-destruct through poor choices."

We were sobered by his comments. I reflected on what the man and his wife had been through over the years. Here was a noble soul, married to a delightful woman after his own good heart. They were not perfect as parents, but it could never be said that they hadn't done their best. They were always at church, held regular family home evenings, and participated in family scripture study and family prayer. Mom and Dad supported their children at school events, athletic events, and cultural events. Several of the children had turned out fine, but a couple of them had serious struggles—drug abuse, dishonesty, and bouts with the law. I had watched over the years as the buffetings of life and the challenges of child rearing had etched their scars into the countenances of these two godly people. I had watched them try to stay positive, try to face what seemed at the time insurmountable hurdles, and I knew something of what they felt. There was no bitterness, no lashing out, no desire to curse God, no tendency to give up and throw in the towel, only resignation to life's opposition and a willingness to keep going, with God's help, in spite of their anguish.

It is inevitable that righteous parents, those who have really tried to lead and guide and walk beside their little ones, will first point the finger of blame at themselves when their hopes for their children do not materialize. "What happened? What did we do wrong? What could we have done differently? Perhaps if our home evenings had been a little more effective, our prayers a little more regular, our family activities more fun, this would not have happened." And so on and so on. Whenever things do not turn out as we planned, we automatically scramble about, frantically searching for answers to hard questions. We know of the promises of the prophets. We know the counsel of the scriptures. "Train up a child in the way he should go," the Bible teaches, "and when he is old, he will not depart from it" (Proverbs 22:6). Thus if one of ours departs from the way of the Lord, the only rational answer seems to be that we did not train him or her in the proper way. What other option is there?

Surely all of us could do our jobs better, could teach and train and lead more effectively, could be more patient, more loving, and more exemplary parents. As long as we are human, we will forevermore fall short of what might be. But there is another variable, one over which we do not have complete control. It is agency, the moral agency of our children. One of the shocking realizations in life is that our little ones do not necessarily inherit all of our commitment, our steadfastness, or our tenacity to hold to the iron rod. Nor do they automatically feel about the restored gospel as we do, no matter how avidly we strive to teach, testify, and exemplify Christian living. I was stopped short in a private interview with one of my own teenagers several years ago by the following: "But Dad, you don't understand; just because you believe this stuff doesn't mean that I believe it in the same way. You see, I simply don't know like you know." I looked into the eyes of my precious child. There was no defiance, no rebellion, only honesty. The unspoken part of the message was: "Dad, I'm trying to have a testimony as deep as yours, but I just don't have one yet. Will you please be patient with me?"

For years I wrestled to understand the meaning of the parable of the ten virgins as recorded in Matthew 25. The message seemed so counter to all that the Master had taught. Why couldn't the wise virgins just share their oil? If each one contributed just a little, I reasoned, perhaps some of the foolish ones could make it to the wedding to meet the bridegroom. And then experience taught me the answer to my query. While I was serving as a priesthood leader, a husband and wife came to see me. They were both distressed about their marriage and family; things seemed to be coming apart in their lives. "How can I help?" I asked. "We need more spirituality in our home," the wife answered. I asked a few questions. "How often do you pray as a family?" They answered that their schedules precluded any kind of family prayer. "Have you been able to hold family home evening?" "Bill and I bowl on Monday nights" was the response. "Do you read the scriptures as a family and as individuals?" The husband answered: "Reading hurts my eyes." "Well, then, how can I help you?" Again the reply: "We want the Spirit in our lives."

It was as though they were saying to me, "Brother Millet, could you reach down into your heart and lend us five years of daily prayer, ten years of regular scripture study, and fifteen years of family spiritual activities?" I couldn't do it. I realized dramatically that there are some things we simply cannot share. Spiritual growth is an individual matter. It is highly personal. As a parent I can bear testimony, live my religion, encourage my children to search and ponder and pray, but in the end the depth of their testimony and the level of their commitment will be largely a product of their own choosing. The exercise of agency can be painful.

Alma the Elder must have agonized as he watched his son Alma seek to destroy the Church. Feelings of personal pain, combined with the piercing embarrassment associated with his own son's flouting of principles of truth, must have resulted in long and sleepless nights. Though the text is silent on this point, if Alma the Elder was a typical parent, the question must have crossed his mind at least once: "How can I remain president of the Church with my family problems? How can I stand before the people, preach righteousness, and call the Saints to repentance, when I cannot control my own son's behavior?" And perhaps he was tortured by the painful thought: "How can I, who am so woefully ineffective with my own son, counsel parents to teach their children and bring them up in light and truth?" Some of us have shared Alma's soul-cries, have experienced the anguish of wanting to do what's right and being called to lead others, only to butt up against the harsh reality of our own wandering child. Alma the Younger must have had similar feelings when his son Corianton forsook the ministry and fell into immoral paths. "Behold, O my son, how great iniquity ye brought upon the Zoramites; for when they saw your conduct they would not believe in my words" (Alma 39:11).

Thankfully God accomplishes his perfect purposes through imperfect people. If only those who had done all things well and who had no personal or family problems were called upon to lead, we would have many fewer leaders in this Church. We all struggle with different things, and the Lord knows about that. The Almighty God himself was not spared the consequences of maintaining moral agency among his sons and daughters; the revelations declare that the heavens wept over the disaffection of Lucifer and one-third of all the spirit sons and daughters of God (see D&C 76:26). As Enoch the seer looked forward in time, he beheld the horrors of the days of Noah and of the consummate wickedness attending the universal flood. "And it came to pass that the God of heaven looked upon the residue of the people, and he wept; and Enoch bore record of it, saying: How is it that the heavens weep, and shed forth their tears as the rain upon the mountains? And Enoch said unto the Lord: How is it that thou canst weep, seeing thou art holy, and from all eternity to all eternity?" It appears that Enoch could not quite grasp why the heavens should weep over the loss of wicked people. After all, he reasoned, God has myriads of creations: "And were it possible that man could number the particles of the earth, yea, millions of earths like this, it would not be a beginning to the number of thy creations" (Moses 7:28–30).

And then Enoch learned something about God—that his infinity does not preclude either his immediacy or his intimacy: "And yet thou art there, and thy bosom is there; and also thou art just; thou art merciful and kind forever." He learned that God is in the business of people, that men and women are his greatest concern, not because they are objects of creation but because they are his very own children. Note the poignancy of this explanation from a Father filled with tender regard: "Behold these thy brethren; they are the workmanship of mine own hands, and I gave unto them their knowledge, in the day I created them; and in the Garden of Eden, gave I unto man his agency; and unto thy brethren have I said, and also given commandment, that they should love one another, and that they should choose me, their Father; but behold, they are without affection, and they hate their own blood . . . , and misery shall be their doom; and the whole heavens shall weep over them, even all the workmanship of mine hands; wherefore should not the heavens weep, seeing these shall suffer?" (Moses 7:30, 32-33, 37). Indeed, what parent, mortal or immortal, does not weep, knowing that his children will suffer? It comes with the turf. We suffer because we care, and the only way to take pain and suffering out of child rearing is to take love out of family relationships.

## Judge Not

My wife, Shauna, was talking with a friend one morning when the conversation turned to children. The woman spoke rather unkindly about a family she knew and of the problems some of the daughters had had. "What kind of parents would let their children do such things?" the woman asked very pointedly. My wife timidly suggested that we really ought not make those kinds of judgments. The woman replied, "No, what I mean is, there's no way my children would ever do those things." Shauna responded, "I hope you're right. But I wouldn't say that if I were you. Children can change overnight."

It's so easy to jump to premature (and often inaccurate) conclusions when we know so little and have available so few of the facts. It's natural to attribute motivation, assign intent, and designate guilt when we really have no idea what's going on in the souls of other people. It is likely that few Latter-day Saint parents who bounce their little ones on their lap, read scriptures with them, kneel in prayer with them, and diligently try to embody the principles of the gospel ever suppose that their children could grow up to be indifferent or hostile toward sacred or eternal things. But sometimes things just don't work out as we plan.

We must learn to rejoice with mothers and fathers whose children excel and whose loved ones develop into model citizens. We must learn to feel deep gratitude for the young ones who are not our own but whose lives bless the lives of their parents and grandparents. On the other hand, we must, as a part of our Christian covenant, be "willing to bear one another's burdens, that they may be light; yea, and . . . willing to mourn with those that mourn; yea, and comfort those that stand in need of comfort" (Mosiah 18:8–9).

It is a wrenching thing to lose a loved one to death. It is perhaps even more wrenching to lose a loved one to the influences of the world, to watch helplessly as one over whom we have prayed and longed and yearned turns a deaf ear to counsel and wanders away into the mists of darkness.

It seems so natural to show up on the doorstep of a friend whose child has been taken in death and grieve with our friends in their loss. It seems so much more difficult to respond in like fashion when our friend's child has gone inactive, has turned to drugs, or has become immoral. We would never think of criticizing a parent whose baby daughter contracted leukemia and died, but we are tempted to place blame at the door of a parent whose son or daughter breaks the law and seems to have died spiritually.

It is a sin against charity and a crime against human decency to ignore or belittle or speak unkindly—to judge—those whose children stray. I believe God will hold us accountable if we do so. Mormon warned: "Wherefore, take heed, . . . that ye do not judge that which is evil to be of God, or that which is good and of God to be of the devil" (Moroni 7:14). Likewise, Alma counseled: "Therefore, . . . see that you are merciful unto your brethren; deal justly, judge righteously, and do good continually; and if ye do all these things then shall ye receive your reward; yea, ye shall have mercy restored unto you again; ye shall have justice restored unto you again; ye shall have a righteous judgment restored unto you again; and ye shall have good rewarded unto you again. For that which ye do send out shall return unto you again, and be restored" (Alma 41:14–15). Maybe there is not much we can do; we probably cannot turn our neighbor's child around on our own. But we can care. We can hurt with our brothers and sisters. And we can pray for them. That's a start. Catchy clichés and platitudes seldom bring comfort, but genuine expressions of love and concern do much to ease the burdens of troubled hearts.

We can be Christians, followers of the lowly Nazarene who ate and drank with sinners. We can reach out, welcome people back, and help them feel the warmth and security they once knew. Alma the Younger took a major detour. But he returned and was welcomed back. Corianton left the strait and narrow path for a time, but he came back. He repented sincerely and was allowed to continue his ministry. He labored faithfully thereafter in the Church (see Alma 49:29–30; 63:10). We can be forgiving and allow people to change. If Johnny strays from the path for a few years and disqualifies himself for a mission but eventually returns to the path, we can greet him joyfully. God can forgive him, and so must we. If Jennifer leaves the strait and

narrow, loses her virtue, has a baby out of wed-
lock, but chooses eventually to come back to
church, we can rejoice in her return. God can
forgive her, and so must we. When people have
repented, they want desperately to put the past
behind them; we as followers of Christ are
under covenant to help them do so. In short, if
loved ones wander for a time, miss some glorious opportunities and forfeit some blessings, we
can still run to meet them while they are yet a
great way off (see Luke 15:20). That they can be
forgiven, that they can have their sins remitted,
is an indication that they can yet inherit the
celestial kingdom. Humble followers of Christ
will treat them, and their parents, accordingly.

That spirit is illustrated in an incident related
by Elder Boyd K. Packer: "A few years ago, it was
my sad privilege to accompany President
Kimball, then President of the Twelve, to a distant stake to replace a stake leader who had
been excommunicated for a transgression. Our
hearts went out to this good man who had
done such an unworthy thing. His sorrow and

anguish and suffering brought to my mind the phrase 'gall of bitterness.'

"Thereafter, on intermittent occasions, I would receive a call from President Kimball: 'Have you heard from this brother? How is he doing? Have you been in touch with him?' After Brother Kimball became President of the Church, the calls did not cease. They increased in frequency.

"One day I received a call from the President. 'I have been thinking of this brother. Do you think it is too soon to have him baptized?' (Always a question, never a command.) I responded with my feelings, and he said, 'Why don't you see if he could come here to see you? If you feel good about it after an interview, we could proceed.'

"A short time later, I arrived very early at the office. As I left my car I saw President Kimball enter his. He rolled down the window to greet me, and I told him I had good news about our brother. 'He was baptized last night,' I said.

"He motioned for me to get into the car and sit beside him and asked me to tell him all about it. I told him of the interview and that I had concluded by telling our brother very plainly that his baptism must not be a signal that his priesthood blessings would be restored in the foreseeable future. I told him that it would be a long, long time before that would happen.

"President Kimball patted me on the knee in a gentle gesture of correction and said, 'Well, maybe not so long . . .' Soon thereafter the intermittent phone calls began again" (*Let Not Your Heart Be Troubled*, 118–19).

"God does not look on sin with allowance," the Prophet Joseph Smith explained, "but when men have sinned, there must be allowance made for them.

"All the religious world is boasting of righteousness: it is the doctrine of the devil to retard the human mind, and hinder our progress, by filling us with self-righteousness. The nearer we get to our heavenly Father, the more we are disposed to look with compassion on perishing souls; we feel that we want to take them upon our shoulders, and cast their sins behind our backs" (Smith, *Teachings of the Prophet Joseph Smith,*

240–41). "Through the history of the generations of man," President Gordon B. Hinckley declared, "the actions of rebellious children have been ladened with sorrow and heartbreak, but even when there has been rebellion, the strong cords of family life have reached out to encircle the rebellious one" (in Conference Report, Apr. 1991, 95).

There is yet another area in which we must not judge or condemn, and it is a different angle on the same problem. Parents who have had wandering children are more than eager (and grateful) to welcome back the straying one. They may also be a bit impatient with siblings who are not as excited and welcoming as Mom and Dad. Let's face the facts: it's tough for a child who is honestly trying to live his or her religion to watch the rebellious son or daughter destroy the home, chase away the peace of the family, make emotional basket cases of their parents, get all the time and most of the family resources, and still feel loving, accepting, and tender toward the prodigal. It's one thing to preach and teach that we ought to be ever ready to forgive; it's another thing to be able to do so. It usually takes some time for the wounds to heal, and "faithful children" and parents may both need to exercise patience and understanding in the process.

A dear friend of mine shared the following experience. At a time when he and his wife were suffering over a wandering child, he prayed and prayed for the strength and the heart to love his errant son, no matter what. That was terribly difficult, for he desperately wanted this boy to become all that the father knew he could become. He wanted to be honest with his son, so he prepared and waited for a time when he felt his expressions could be heartfelt and genuine. On one occasion he waited up for his son until about two o'clock in the morning, when the son came in. The father said, "Come in, Bill. Let's talk for a moment." The young man backpeddled. "I know I'm late. I know I said I would be in earlier." The father cut him off. "No, no, Bill. That's not what I wanted to talk with you about. I just wanted to tell you that I've missed you. It's been a long time since we sat down and spent a few moments together. Do you have some time right now?" Startled, the son said, "I guess so."

"Bill," the father continued, "I need to tell you something, and it's really important to me that I say just what I'm feeling. I know that for the time being you have chosen to travel another direction, to go in a different path than the rest of the family has chosen to take. I would be lying if I said anything other than it hurts your mom and me deeply to see you go this way. But I've come to realize something in the past few days. As much as I want you to be active and involved in the Church—and I want that more than anything in the world—that decision has to be yours. And so I want you to know even if you should decide that you never again want to be associated with the Church, we'll still love you, love you with all our hearts. You're our son, and you'll always be our son. And nothing will ever change that."

Bill was touched by the honesty of his father and, more especially, by the rich outpouring of a love now devoid of rules and conditions. Through tears, my friend explained that that

moment was a turning point in their relationship.

Our family pain may best be faced with perspective, particularly the perspective provided
by the great plan of happiness. On occasions
when I have been most discouraged by family
matters, I have engaged in two essential activities.

First of all, I have spent a great deal of time
on my knees. A petition in the Book of Mormon
has taken on new meaning for me. Alma and his
missionary companions were stunned by the
perverseness and apostasy of the Zoramites.
After expressing to God his utter disgust with
their pride and idolatry, Alma prayed: "O Lord,
wilt thou give me strength, that I may bear with
mine infirmities. For I am infirm, and such
wickedness among this people doth pain my
soul. O Lord, my heart is exceedingly sorrowful;
wilt thou comfort my soul in Christ" (Alma
31:30–31). Prayer becomes a means of gaining
comfort, additional strength to bear up under
our burdens, and divine direction in dealing
with specific problems.

Second, I have spent many hours in the temple, the site of intersection between heaven and earth, the holy place where we can come unto God. The temple provides perspective on time and eternity. It serves for me as a gentle slap in the face, a sobering reminder of what matters most. I may come into the temple with what seems an unbearable burden—concerns about finances, children, or church matters. I may not leave the temple with any more money in my pocket or even an idea of how to come up with more (though such things do happen). I may not understand any more clearly how to deal with a rebellious youngster (though certain impressions may come). And I may not know exactly who should be called as the Relief Society president or the Scoutmaster (though such knowledge does come to us on occasion). But almost always I leave the temple built up, strengthened, fortified in what must be done. My mind and heart have been refocused on eternal things. Covenants. Ordinances. Family. Sealing power. Righteousness. There is consummate peace to be found in perspective.

The hope of which the scriptures speak is not just wanting good things to happen. Hope is a settled condition, a rest and a peace that allow us to proceed confidently in the midst of turmoil. It comes to us by the power of the Holy Ghost, who is the Comforter. Elder M. Russell Ballard stated: "Many feel helpless to deal with the chaos that seems to prevail in the world. Others anguish over family members who are being carried downstream in a swift, raging current of weakening values and declining moral standards. Children particularly are suffering as society drifts further and further away from the commandments of God.

"Many have even resigned themselves to accept the wickedness and cruelty of the world as being irreparable. They have given up hope. They have decided to quit trying to make the world a better place in which they and their families can live. They have surrendered to despair.

"Admittedly we have ample reason to be deeply concerned because we see no immediate answers to the seemingly unsolvable problems confronting the human family. But regardless of this dark picture, which will ultimately get worse, we must never allow ourselves to give up hope! Moroni, having seen our day, counseled, 'Wherefore, there must be faith; and if there must be faith there must also be hope' (Moroni 10:20)" (in Conference Report, Oct. 1992, 42).

To hold on, to hope on in regard to the family is to face life and its challenges with courage and conviction, recognizing that God is in his heaven and knows of our sufferings. To proceed with hope is to live the gospel the best we can, to trust in the infinite power and never-ending mercy of Jesus Christ, and to surrender our burdens to him. Jesus is the Balm of Gilead. His is the soothing ointment that heals the wounds of the brokenhearted. To a degree, we each have wandered, just as do some of our children. "All we like sheep have gone astray; we have turned every one to his own way" (Isaiah 53:6). But thanks be to God, "he hath borne our griefs, and carried our sorrows" (Isaiah 53:4). Because he has taken upon him our infirmities, he is filled with mercy and knows how to succor his people according to their individual needs (see Alma 7:12).

Truly, anything upon which Christ places his hand is healed—individual, family, or nation. The Savior may not take away our problems, and he certainly will not shield us from all pain, but he will provide us perspective and strength to bear up under them. As we submit cheerfully and patiently to the will of the Lord, he will "ease the burdens which are put upon your shoulders, that even you cannot feel them upon your backs, . . . that ye may know of a surety that I, the Lord God, do visit my people in their afflictions" (Mosiah 24:14).

# WITHIN THE COVENANT

W e are a people of covenant. In fact, whenever our Heavenly Father has had a people on earth to whom he has revealed himself and the truths and powers of salvation, he has always done so through covenant. He promises to make of us "a chosen generation, a royal priesthood, an holy nation, a peculiar people." We promise to abide by the terms and obligations of the covenant, namely, to "shew forth the praises of him who hath called [us] out of darkness into his marvellous light" (1 Peter 2:9). The God of heaven has restored the fulness of his gospel in our day so that his everlasting covenant might be reestablished on earth (see D&C 1:22). Indeed, the gospel of Jesus Christ represents the "new and an everlasting covenant" (D&C 22.1, 45.9, 49:9; 66.2, 133.57): *everlasting* in that it has been on the earth from the beginning of time; *new* in that it is restored anew following periods of apostasy. The Savior's commission to an early Latter-day Saint is just as applicable to us who live at the end of the age: "Thou shalt preach the fulness of my gospel, which I have sent forth in these last days, the covenant which I have sent forth to recover my people, which are of the house of Israel" (D&C 39:11).

## A Premortal Covenant People

Central to Latter-day Saint theology is the mind-expanding concept that we lived before we came here; the doctrine of the premortal existence of men and women is fundamental to our faith. Very little of what we do and feel and accomplish in our second estate may be comprehended independent of what we did and who we were in our first estate. Alma teaches us that many of us demonstrated "exceeding faith and good works" in the premortal existence as a preparation for the callings and assignments we would receive here (Alma 13:3).

Following our birth as spirits, being endowed with agency, each of the spirit sons and daughters of God grew and developed and progressed according to our desires for truth and righteousness. "Being subject to law," Elder Bruce R. McConkie wrote, "and having their agency, all the spirits of men, while yet in the Eternal

Presence, developed aptitudes, talents, capacities, and abilities of every sort, kind, and degree. During the long expanse of life which then was, an infinite variety of talents and abilities came into being. As the ages rolled, no two spirits remained alike. . . . Abraham and Moses and all of the prophets sought and obtained the talent for spirituality. Mary and Eve were two of the greatest of all the spirit daughters of the Father. The whole house of Israel, known and segregated out from their fellows, was inclined toward spiritual things" (*Mortal Messiah*, 1:23).

Perhaps the greatest foreordination—based on premortal faithfulness—is foreordination to lineage and family: individuals come to earth through a designated lineage that entitles them to remarkable blessings, but also a lineage that carries with it burdens and responsibilities. As a people, therefore, we enjoy "a type of collective foreordination—a selection of spirits to form an entire favored group or lineage." Yet, "it is a collective foreordination [that] is nonetheless based on individual premortal faithfulness and spiritual capacity" (*Life Before*, 144). In the words of

Elder Melvin J. Ballard, Israel is "a group of souls tested, tried, and proven before they were born into the world. . . . Through this lineage were to come the true and tried souls that had demonstrated their righteousness in the spirit world before they came here" (*Melvin J. Ballard*, 218–19).

"Remember the days of old," Moses counseled his people, "consider the years of many generations: ask thy father, and he will shew thee; thy elders, and they will tell thee. When the most High divided to the nations their inheritance, when he separated the sons of Adam, he set the bounds of the people according to the number of the children of Israel. For the Lord's portion is his people; Jacob is the lot of his inheritance" (Deuteronomy 32:7–9). In speaking to the Athenians, the apostle Paul declared: "God that made the world and all things therein, . . . hath made of one blood all nations of men for to dwell on all the face of the earth, and hath determined the times before appointed, and the bounds of their habitation" (Acts 17:24, 26).

President Harold B. Lee explained: "Those born to the lineage of Jacob, who was later to be called Israel, and his posterity, who were known as the children of Israel, were born into the most illustrious lineage of any of those who came upon the earth as mortal beings.

"All these rewards were seemingly promised, or foreordained, before the world was. Surely these matters must have been determined by the kind of lives we had lived in that premortal spirit world. Some may question these assumptions, but at the same time they will accept without any question the belief that each one of us will be judged when we leave this earth according to his or her deeds during our lives here in mortality. Isn't it just as reasonable to believe that what we have received here in this earth [life] was given to each of us according to the merits of our conduct before we came here?" (in Conference Report, Oct. 1973, 7–8).

It thus appears that the declaration of lineage by patriarchs is as much a statement as to who and what we were as it is who we are now and what we may become. There are those, of course, who believe otherwise, those who propose that premortality has little or nothing to do with mortality, that there is no tie between faithfulness there and lineage and station here; to believe in any other way, they contend, is racist or exclusivistic. In my view, if there is no relationship between the first estate and the second, why should I believe there is any relationship between what I do here and what I will receive hereafter?

Who are we, then? President Lee declared: "You are all the sons and daughters of God. Your spirits were created and lived as organized intelligences before the world was. You have been blessed to have a physical body because of your obedience to certain commandments in that premortal state. You are now born into a family to which you have come, into the nations through which you have come, as a reward for the kind of lives you lived before you came here and at a time in the world's history, as the Apostle Paul taught the men of Athens and as the Lord revealed to Moses, determined by the faithfulness of each of those who lived before this world was created" (in Conference Report, Oct. 1973, 7). And yet coming to earth through a peculiar lineage involves much more than boasting of a blessing; it entails bearing a burden. "Once we know who we are," Elder Russell M. Nelson said, "and the royal lineage of which we are a part, our actions and directions in life will be more appropriate to our inheritance" ("Thanks for the Covenant," 59).

## The Covenant in Mortality

Those who come to the earth through the lineage of Abraham, Isaac, and Jacob do so with an inner attraction toward light and truth; they have a predisposition to receive the truth and abide by that truth. They may in fact choose in mortality to turn a deaf ear to the message of the gospel or to the principles of righteousness; they may harden their hearts and close their minds and thereby live beneath their spiritual privileges (see Alma 13:4). But if they hearken to the Light of Christ and follow their consciences, they shall, either in this life or in the next, be led to the higher light of the Holy Ghost found in the covenant gospel (see D&C 84:46–48; see also Smith, *Gospel Doctrine*, 67–68; McConkie, *New Witness*, 260–61).

Receiving the gospel, the priesthood, and opportunities for eternal reward in this life is no coincidence; we have come to earth at a designated time. The blessings of the covenant are available to us here and now as a part of an eternal plan. On the day of Pentecost, the apostle Peter set forth the principles that those who had been touched by the Spirit must follow in order to be saved: "Repent, and be baptized every one of you in the name of Jesus Christ for the remission of sins, and ye shall receive the gift of the Holy Ghost. For the promise is unto you, and to your children, and to all that are afar off, even as many as the Lord our God shall call" (Acts 2:38–39). The Prophet Joseph Smith said of that passage from the New Testament: "By this we learn that the promise of the Holy Ghost is made unto as many as those to whom the doctrine of repentance was to be preached, which was unto all nations. And we discover also, that the promise was to extend by lineage; for Peter says, not only unto you, but 'to your children, and to all that are afar off.' From this we infer, that the promise was to continue unto their children's children, and even unto as many as the Lord their God should call" (Smith, *Teachings of the Prophet Joseph Smith*, 81).

To be of the house of Israel, to be of the chosen lineage, and to open oneself to greater light and knowledge and thereby continue the eternal quest is to be possessed of believing blood. "Latter-day Saints need to believe," Elder Loren C. Dunn explained. "They need to take every opportunity to develop faith, both in their own lives and in the lives of others.

"Faith is a part of our heritage. Those who embrace the gospel of Jesus Christ are the blood of Israel, and characteristic of the house of Israel is the ability to believe. Some have referred to it as 'believing blood'" (in Conference Report, Apr. 1981, 35–36). Or, as Elder Bruce R. McConkie observed: "What then is believing blood? It is the blood that flows in the veins of those who are the literal seed of Abraham—not that the blood itself believes, but that those born in that lineage have both the right and a special spiritual capacity to recognize, receive, and believe the truth. The term is simply a beautiful, a poetic, and a symbolic way of referring to the seed of Abraham to whom the promises were made. It identifies those who developed in pre-existence the talent to recognize the truth and to desire righteousness" (*New Witness*, 38–39).

In short, what we were and what we did greatly affect what we are and what we do now. We cannot escape now who we once were or how and in what manner we previously opened ourselves to the goodness of God and his divine plan. President Joseph F. Smith thus taught that "our knowledge of persons and things before we came here, combined with the divinity awakened within our souls through obedience to the gospel, powerfully affects, in my opinion, all our likes and dislikes, and guides our preferences in the course of this life, provided we give careful heed to the admonitions of the Spirit.

"All those salient truths which come home so forcibly to the head and heart seem but the awakening of the memories of the spirit. Can we know anything here that we did not know before we came? . . . But in coming here, we forgot all, that our agency might be free indeed, to choose good or evil, that we might merit the reward of our own choice and conduct. But by the power of the Spirit, in the redemption of Christ, through obedience, we often catch a spark from the awakened memories of the immortal soul, which lights up our whole being as with the glory of our former home" (*Gospel Doctrine*, 12–14).

We speak of those who come to earth through the lineage of parents who have been married in the temple as having been "born in the covenant." What a majestic manner in which to describe the situation of those who enter upon life in the covenant gospel. Those who are sealed in the temple to faithful parents are entitled to the very same privileges—the right to inherit and possess, as heirs, as though they had been born in the covenant. There is power in the covenant. There is protection in the covenant. There is direction in the covenant. There is purpose in the covenant. I have watched with much interest over the years as a temple marriage has literally transformed men and women, refined them, and fashioned them into Saints of God. I have watched with similar interest as little children have exulted in the warmth, the security, and the staying power of a home built upon and operated according to covenant. Jesus our Lord is the Mediator of the Covenant, and it is Jesus who places his healing and enabling hand upon husbands and wives, parents and children who are striving to be true to their covenants. "It may be asked," said President Joseph Fielding Smith, "what is the advantage coming to those born under the covenant? Being *heirs* they have claims on the blessings of the gospel beyond what those not so born are entitled to receive. They may receive a greater guidance, a greater protection, a greater inspiration from the Spirit of the Lord" (*Doctrines of Salvation,* 2:90).

My grandfather joined the Church near New Orleans, Louisiana. He and my grandmother sought to raise my father and his three brothers in the Church. By the time I was born, my father was not active in the Church. My mother was a Methodist, though she loved the Church and its members and enjoyed being a part of the

Mormon life. My Uncle Joseph and Aunt Gladys were very instrumental in my mother's baptism and in our activation as a family over the next several years. I can still remember the long drive to the Salt Lake Temple, the excitement Mom and Dad displayed about our family being sealed together, and the feelings of anticipation in my own young heart (I was about eleven).

It is hard for me to put in words the surge of sweet emotion that came into my heart as I saw the Salt Lake Temple for the first time. Something deep within the recesses of my soul whispered that this was a holy setting, and that what was about to take place with my family would have long-lasting effects. I did not understand much of what I saw and heard that day, but the Spirit of the Lord confirmed to me that my family would never again be the same. And so it was. Mom and Dad were kinder to each other and to us. We talked frequently over the years about the continuation of the family in eternity and of the need for each of us to do our part to secure our love and associations forever. I now look back and realize that it was the power of covenant, the new and everlasting covenant, that entered like a fire into our home and into my heart. It had a transforming effect on Mom and Dad; they worked tirelessly and consecrated themselves sincerely to building the kingdom and establishing Zion, both in our home and in the Church. I learned by observation what it meant to give oneself to a cause. I learned what it meant to build a life on covenants and ordinances. In the process, a firm foundation was laid for my own life. The Almighty has truly placed upon me "the testimony of the covenant" (D&C 109:38).

While I was serving as a bishop some years ago, a mother and her two children joined the Church. They were enthusiastic beyond description about their newfound faith and dived in as deeply as they could. The father of the family, however, was not baptized and was not exactly excited about his family's decision. After being in the Church for several months, the mother asked to visit with me. She said, "I think it's time for me to get a divorce. My husband, Fred, not only refuses to get serious about Mormonism but he has now limited my church attendance. He told me yesterday that I could choose which one of the three meetings on Sunday I wanted to attend, but that I was only allowed one hour per week of religion." I didn't know her husband very well, but it seemed that divorce was not the answer. I suggested that she be obedient to her husband for the time being to hold the family together, that she fast and pray regularly for his heart to be softened, and that she do everything in her power to "make home like church." She didn't know what I meant, and so I explained that she ought to be as Christlike and positive and loving as she could genuinely be and show him just how great a difference the gospel of Jesus Christ had made in their lives.

Not much progress seemed to be made in the months that followed. In fact, I remember standing at the pulpit on the day that their eight-year-old was baptized. I was speaking on the importance of entering the Lord's kingdom through baptism and of the vital place of the Holy Ghost in our lives. I turned in the direction of the father of the family as I was bearing my testimony, only to receive the most bitter, angry, and hateful stare I had ever received. The father actually got up before I had finished and stormed out of the chapel. I thought to myself, "If ever there was a rebellious soul in all the world, we have one here. If ever there was a scoundrel rotten to the core, we have one here. This clown doesn't have enough decency to sit through a thirty-minute meeting in order to make his little boy happy. If ever a woman was entitled to a divorce and some peace of mind, we have one here." I am not proud of my feelings on that occasion. To be honest, if anyone had suggested to me that this pitiful excuse for a man would ever amount to anything, I would have laughed. It is perhaps an indication of my lack of judgment, Christianity, and general perception that the right missionaries eventually came to town, touched this man, baptized him, and set him on course. It was then especially sweet to watch him prepare for and receive the ordinances of the temple, return frequently with his sweetheart, and become a new creature in Christ. He was transformed by gospel covenants

and ordinances. His family was similarly transformed. Sarcasm was replaced by sweetness.
Macho man was replaced by priesthood man, a
man of covenant. Whereas before he had ruled
his family with an iron hand, he now led
lovingly with the rod of iron, the word of God.
He is now a gentle and kindly soul who reflects
the ways and works of the Master, and a dear
and valued friend. There is power in the
covenant, consummate power to lift and bless
and reorient.

Celestial marriage is so much more than a
lovely social custom, so much more than a
Mormon tradition. It is a means of perpetuating
the everlasting covenant from generation to generation, of linking the Lord's chosen people by
sacred ordinance. It is the means whereby "the
promises made to the fathers" (D&C 2:2) are
realized in the hearts and lives of the children.
Covenants are fundamental, and to the degree
that Latter-day Saints take seriously the counsel
of modern apostles and prophets to simplify,
reduce, and prioritize, they take seriously the
obligation to focus on covenants.

Those who through no fault of their own are abandoned by a spouse's violation of the covenant or by divorce can through their own faithful obedience anticipate all the blessings of the covenant—if not here, then hereafter. The privilege of eternal marriage may not come again in this sphere, but the powers of the covenant can, like a broad umbrella, shield and protect and embrace the God-fearing. Righteousness is the key. Faithfulness is paramount. Our God, who is a God of justice as well as of mercy, knows the hearts of all of us and will not deprive us of eternal privileges because of the sins of others. Further, as President Lorenzo Snow affirmed, "There is no Latter-day Saint who dies after having lived a faithful life who will lose anything because of having failed to do certain things when opportunities were not furnished him or her. In other words, if a young man or a young woman has no opportunity of getting married, and they live faithful lives up to the time of their death, they will have all the blessings, exaltation, and glory that any man or woman will have who had this opportunity and improved it. That is sure and positive" (*Teachings of Lorenzo Snow*, 138).

"We are . . . children of the covenant," Elder Russell M. Nelson declared. "We have received, as did they of old, the holy priesthood and the everlasting gospel. Abraham, Isaac, and Jacob are our ancestors. We are of Israel. We have the right to receive the gospel, blessings of the priesthood, and eternal life. Nations of the earth will be blessed by our efforts and by the labors of our posterity. The literal seed of Abraham and those who are gathered into his family by adoption receive these promised blessings— predicated upon acceptance of the Lord and obedience to his commandments" (in Conference Report, Apr. 1995, 42–43).

It is essential that members of the Church, young and old, know that they are the sons and daughters of an Eternal Heavenly Father and, with Christ our Exemplar, heir to all that the Father has. It is also vital that each one of us knows his or her place in the royal family as a literal descendant of Abraham, Isaac, and Jacob: we are heirs to the promises made to them. The covenants into which we enter in this life are mortal reminders of premortal promises. They point us toward our distant past and prepare us for a glorious future. When our eyes are focused on covenants, our eyes are likewise single to the glory of God. Elder Boyd K. Packer highlighted the importance of being a covenant people:

"Several years ago I installed a stake president in England. . . . He had an unusual sense of direction. He was like a mariner with a sextant who took his bearings from the stars. I met with him each time he came to conference and was impressed that he kept himself and his stake on course.

"Fortunately for me, when it was time for his release, I was assigned to reorganize the stake. It was then that I discovered what that sextant was and how he adjusted it to check his position and get a bearing for himself and for his members.

"He accepted his release, and said: 'I was happy to accept the call to serve as stake president, and I am equally happy to accept my release. I did not serve just because I was under *call.* I served because I am under *covenant.* And I can keep my covenants quite as well as a home teacher as I can serving as stake president."

"This president understood the word *covenant.*

"While he was neither a scriptorian nor a gospel scholar, he somehow had learned that exaltation is achieved by keeping covenants, not by holding high position.

"The mariner gets his bearing from light coming from celestial bodies—the sun by day, the stars by night. That stake president did not need a mariner's sextant to set his course. In his mind there was a sextant infinitely more refined and precise than any mariner's instrument.

"The spiritual sextant, which each of us has, also functions on the principle of light from celestial sources. Set that sextant in your mind to the word *covenant* or the word *ordinance.* The light will come through. Then you can fix your position and set a true course in life" (in Conference Report, Apr. 1987, 26–27).

# THE SEALING AND
# BINDING POWERS

E lder Boyd K. Packer related the following story: "Some time ago I was counseling a woman who had joined the Church following the breakup of her marriage and the loss of her only child, a boy who was nine years old at the time he passed away. She told me something that I remember very well because it touched me deeply.

"After the separation in her marriage, while she was trying to make a living for herself and her son, he became afflicted with a terminal disease. Some time before he passed away, he became aware of the fact that he was not going to live. His mother said from that time on he had only one thing on his mind: over and over again he would say pleadingly, 'Mama, you won't forget me, will you? I won't be forgotten, will I?' The pleading of a dying youngster speaks somehow for all of us, and expresses our yearning not to be forgotten" (*That All May Be Edified*, 172).

If in fact the family is the most important unit in time and eternity, we would suppose that God has made provision, from the beginning down into our own day, for its perpetuation and continuation. And so he has. Not one of us will be forgotten, and not one of us need be lost.

## *The Sealing Power Anciently*

After his baptism by water and his quickening by the Spirit, our father Adam "heard a voice out of heaven, saying: Thou art baptized with fire, and with the Holy Ghost. This is the record of the Father, and the Son, from henceforth and forever; and thou art after the order of him who was without beginning of days or end of years, from all eternity to all eternity. Behold, thou art one in me, a son of God; and thus may all become my sons. Amen" (Moses 6:66–68). President Ezra Taft Benson explained: "When our Heavenly Father placed Adam and Eve on this earth, He did so with the purpose in mind of teaching them how to regain His presence. Our Father promised a Savior to redeem them from their fallen condition. He gave to them the plan of salvation and told them to teach their children faith in Jesus Christ and repentance. Further, Adam and his posterity were commanded by God to be baptized, to receive the Holy Ghost, and to enter into the order of the Son of God.

"To enter into the order of the Son of God is the equivalent today of entering into the fullness of the Melchizedek Priesthood, which is only received in the house of the Lord" ("What I Hope You Will Teach Your Children about the Temple," 8).

Abraham wrote that he "sought for the blessings of the fathers, and the right whereunto I should be ordained to administer the same; having been myself a follower of righteousness, desiring also to be one who possessed great knowledge, and to be a greater follower of righteousness, and to possess a greater knowledge, and to be a father of many nations, a prince of peace, and desiring to receive instructions, and to keep the commandments of God, I became a rightful heir, a High Priest, holding the right belonging to the fathers" (Abraham 1:2).

Abraham was ordained by Melchizedek and received from the king of Salem the fulness of the holy priesthood (see D&C 84:14; Smith,

*Words of Joseph Smith*, 246). The Prophet Joseph Smith taught that "those holding the fulness of the Melchizedek Priesthood are kings and priests of the Most High God, holding the keys of power and blessings" (Smith, *Teachings of Joseph Smith*, 322).

That same holy order of God, the power by which men and women are brought into the presence of the Lord, was contained on the first set of tablets that Moses broke when he discovered the wickedness and inability of the Israelites to receive the higher law. Moses was instructed by Jehovah that the second set of tablets "shall not be according to the first, for I will take away the priesthood out of their midst; therefore my holy order, and the ordinances thereof, shall not go before them; for my presence shall not go up in their midst, lest I destroy them" (JST Exodus 34:1; compare JST Deuteronomy 10:1–2). We assume, knowing of the blessings of the temple among them, that this same authority was held by the Nephites from the beginning, that Lehi and Nephi and Jacob and Alma and their successors enjoyed the fulness of the blessings of the priesthood (see 2 Nephi 5:16; Jacob 1:17; 2:2; Mosiah 2:1; Alma 16:13; 3 Nephi 11:1). The Lord's commendation to Nephi, son of Helaman, for his unwearyingness in declaring the word was followed by this announcement: "Behold, I give unto you power, that whatsoever ye shall seal on earth shall be sealed in heaven; and whatsoever ye shall loose on earth shall be loosed in heaven; and thus shall ye have power among this people" (Helaman 10:7). A half century later and a hemisphere away, the Lord Jesus delivered similar priesthood keys and sealing powers, including the fulness of the priesthood, to Simon Peter and the other apostles (see Matthew 16:13–19; 17:1–8; 18:18; Smith, *Teachings of the Prophet Joseph Smith*, 158; Smith, *Words of Joseph Smith*, 246).

Mormon explained that after the Savior visited the Nephites and established the full program of the kingdom of God, "Behold, it came to pass that the people of Nephi did wax strong, and did multiply exceedingly fast, and became an exceedingly fair and delightsome people. And they were married, and given in marriage, and were blessed according to the multitude of the promises which the Lord had made unto them" (4 Nephi 1:10–11). Those promises, the "promises made to the fathers," surely pertained to eternal marriage in holy temples and the sealing and perpetuation of family units into eternity. That right would have continued until the Nephites sinned against light and were destroyed by the Lamanites.

Elder Bruce R. McConkie observed that despite periods of apostasy "there was not so much as the twinkling of an eye during the whole so-called pre-Christian Era when the Church of Jesus Christ was not upon the earth, organized basically in the same way it now is. . . . There was always apostolic power. The Melchizedek Priesthood always directed the course of the Aaronic Priesthood. All of the prophets held a position in the hierarchy of the day. Celestial marriage has always existed. Indeed, such is the heart and core of the Abrahamic covenant. Elias and Elijah came to restore this ancient order and to give the sealing power, which gives it eternal efficacy" ("The Bible," 6; see also Smith, *Doctrines of Salvation*, 3:85).

## *The Keys of the Priesthood Restored*

That which took place on the Mount of Transfiguration just six months before the Crucifixion has its parallel in the latter-day Church. The winter and spring of 1836 were an era of both pentecost and transfiguration. By early April, bearers of the priesthood had undergone the ordinance of washing and anointing. On Sunday, 3 April 1836, one week after the first dedicatory service of the Kirtland Temple, the Saints were again assembled in the house of the Lord. In the morning Elder Thomas B. Marsh, then president of the Quorum of the Twelve Apostles, and Elder David W. Patten were called upon to speak. In the afternoon the First Presidency and the apostles participated in a sacrament service, after which Joseph Smith and Oliver Cowdery knelt in prayer behind drawn curtains adjacent to the large pulpits on the west side of the main floor of the temple. At that moment a wondrous vision burst upon them, one of the great theophanies of the ages.

Jesus the Christ appeared to the president and assistant president of his restored Church. Our Lord's appearance was but the beginning of the realization of his promise given three years earlier: "And inasmuch as my people build a house unto me in the name of the Lord, and do not suffer any unclean thing to come into it, that it be not defiled, my glory shall rest upon it; yea, and my presence shall be there, for I will come into it, and all the pure in heart that shall come into it shall see God" (D&C 97:15–16). The Savior accepted the offering of his Saints—this temple built at great sacrifice—and then expanded their vision of what they had accomplished: "Yea the hearts of thousands and tens of thousands shall greatly rejoice in consequence of the blessings which shall be poured out, and the endowment with which my servants have been endowed in this house" (D&C 110:9).

"After this vision [of the Savior] closed, the heavens were again opened unto us; and Moses appeared before us, and committed unto us the keys of the gathering of Israel from the four parts of the earth, and the leading of the ten tribes from the land of the north" (D&C 110:11). The keys, or directing powers, restored by the ancient lawgiver formalized the work of gathering that had been begun. These keys enabled the Saints to accomplish the directive delivered in September 1830: "And ye are called to bring to pass the gathering of mine elect; for mine elect hear my voice and harden not their hearts" (D&C 29:7). To the president of The Church of Jesus Christ of Latter-day Saints—the man appointed "to preside over the whole church, and to be like unto Moses" (D&C 107:91)—were given keys to gather modern Israel. Even as Moses led ancient Israel out of Egyptian bondage, so the president of the Church was given keys to lead modern Israel out of the bondage of modern Egypt into Zion.

"After this, Elias appeared, and committed the dispensation of the gospel of Abraham, saying that in us and our seed all generations after us should be blessed" (D&C 110:12). The identity of Elias is not given in the revelation. This heavenly

messenger restored the keys necessary to estab-
lish the ancient patriarchal order, making Joseph
Smith and the faithful Saints who receive celestial marriage heirs to the blessings and "promises
made to the fathers"—Abraham, Isaac, and
Jacob. Elias thus restored the power by which
eternal families are organized through the new
and everlasting covenant of marriage. "As the
crowning cause for wonderment," Elder Bruce R.
McConkie explained, "that God who is no
respecter of persons has given a like promise [to
that of Abraham and Joseph Smith] to every
[member] in the kingdom who has gone to the
holy temple and entered into the blessed order
of matrimony there performed. Every person
married in the temple for time and for all eternity has sealed upon him, conditioned upon his
faithfulness, all of the blessings of the ancient
patriarchs, including the crowning promise and
assurance of eternal increase, which means,
literally, a posterity as numerous as the dust
particles of the earth" (*Millennial Messiah*, 264).

"After this vision had closed, another great
and glorious vision burst upon us; for Elijah the

prophet, who was taken to heaven without tasting death, stood before us, and said: Behold, the time has fully come, which was spoken of by the mouth of Malachi—testifying that he [Elijah] should be sent, before the great and dreadful day of the Lord come—to turn the hearts of the fathers to the children, and the children to the fathers, lest the whole earth be smitten with a curse" (D&C 110:13–15). Precisely on the day that Elijah's appearance took place, Jews throughout the world were engaged in the celebration of the Passover. Since the time of Malachi—from about 400 or 500 B.C. until now—Jews worldwide have awaited Elijah's coming with anxious anticipation. Elijah did come but not to Jewish homes; he came rather to a synagogue of the Saints and to his legal administrators on earth. There he bestowed keys of inestimable worth.

When Moroni appeared to Joseph Smith in 1823 he quoted numerous passages from the Old and New Testaments. The Prophet wrote in his official history that Moroni quoted Malachi 4:5–6 but gave a rendering different from that in the King James Version. Malachi (through whom this promise came), we learn from the Prophet, "had his eye fixed on the restoration of the priesthood" (D&C 128:17). The prophecy began: "Behold, I will reveal unto you the Priesthood, by the hand of Elijah the prophet, before the coming of the great and dreadful day of the Lord" (Joseph Smith–History 1:38; D&C 2:1). Joseph and Oliver had been ordained to the Melchizedek Priesthood and been given apostolic power and commission as early as 1829. How was it, then, that Elijah would reveal the priesthood? Simply stated, Elijah was sent in 1836 to reveal, or make known, keys of the priesthood and sealing powers that had not yet been fully understood or were not fully operational in this dispensation, especially in regard to families. Now the power to gather, organize, and seal families was fully functional. Elijah restored the keys whereby families, organized in the patriarchal order through the powers delivered by Elias, could be bound and sealed for eternity.

Three months before his death, Joseph Smith instructed the Latter-day Saints concerning the mission of Elijah: "The spirit, power, and calling of Elijah is, that ye have power to hold the key of the revelations, ordinances, oracles, powers and endowments of the fulness of the Melchizedek Priesthood and of the kingdom of God on the earth" (Smith, *Teachings of the Prophet Joseph Smith*, 337). Elijah restored the keys whereby individuals and families, through the blessings of the holy temple, may develop line upon line to the point that they may receive the fulness of the priesthood and thus become kings and queens, priests and priestesses, unto God in the patriarchal order (see Smith, *Teachings of the Prophet Joseph Smith*, 323). Through the powers delivered by Elias—the new and everlasting covenant of marriage, the order entered into by Abraham, Isaac, and Jacob—eternal families are created, here and hereafter. Through the powers delivered by Elijah, husband and wife may be sealed unto eternal life, for "the power of Elijah is sufficient to make our calling and election sure" (Smith, *Teachings of the Prophet Joseph Smith*, 338).

Elijah came to "plant in the hearts of the children the promises made to the fathers" whereby the "hearts of the children [should] turn to their fathers" (Joseph Smith–History 1:39; D&C 2:2). The Spirit of the Lord witnesses to faithful Latter-day Saints of the central place of eternal marriage and of the sublime joys associated with the everlasting continuation of the family. Through temples, God's promises to the fathers—the promises pertaining to the gospel, the priesthood, and eternal increase (see Abraham 2:8–11)—are extended to all faithful Saints of all ages. The hearts of the children turn to the ancient fathers because the children are now participants in and recipients of the blessings of the fathers. Being profoundly grateful for such privileges, members of the Church, motivated by the spirit of Elijah, also find their hearts turning to their more immediate fathers and do all within their power through family history research and attendant temple work to ensure that the blessings of Abraham, Isaac, and Jacob are enjoyed by ancestry as well as posterity. "If it were not so [that is, if Elijah had not come], the whole earth would be utterly wasted at

[Christ's] coming" (Joseph Smith–History 1:39; D&C 2:3).

Why would the earth be wasted at his coming? Because the earth would not have accomplished its foreordained purpose of establishing on its face a family system patterned after the order of heaven. If there were no sealing powers whereby families could be bound together, then the earth would never "answer the end of its creation" (D&C 49:16). It would be wasted and cursed, for all men and women would be forever without root or branch, without ancestry or posterity. But because Elijah came, all other ordinances for the living and the dead (baptisms, confirmations, ordinations, sealings, and so forth) have real meaning and are of efficacy, virtue, and force in eternity (see Smith, *Teachings of the Prophet Joseph Smith*, 172; see also Smith, *Doctrines of Salvation*, 2:115–28). The ordinances associated with the ministry and bestowal of keys by Moses, Elias, and Elijah, culminating in temples of the Lord, are the capstone blessings of the gospel and the consummation of the Father's work: they provide purpose and perspective for all other gospel principles and ordinances.

As President Ezra Taft Benson explained, "Elijah brought the keys of sealing powers—that power which *seals* a man to a woman and *seals* their posterity to them endlessly, that which *seals* their forefathers to them all the way back to Adam. This is the power and order that Elijah revealed—that *same order* of priesthood which God gave to Adam and to all the ancient patriarchs which followed after him" ("What I Hope You Will Teach Your Children about the Temple," 10). Elder James E. Faust pointed out: "Perhaps we regard the power bestowed by Elijah as something associated only with formal ordinances performed in sacred places. But these ordinances become dynamic and productive of good only as they reveal themselves in our daily lives. Malachi said that the power of Elijah would turn the *hearts* of the fathers and the children to each other. The heart is the seat of the emotions and a conduit for revelation (see Malachi 4:5–6). This sealing power thus reveals itself in family relationships, in attributes and virtues developed in a nurturing environment, and in loving service. These are the cords that bind families together, and the priesthood advances their development" (in Conference Report, Apr. 1993, 47).

The priesthood is the power of God delegated to man on earth to act in all things for the salvation of humankind. It is the power by which the worlds were made, the power by which the sick are healed, the lame made to walk, the blind to see, and the dead to rise again. It is the power by which we enter into covenant and the power by which we participate in the saving ordinances. Where the priesthood of God is, there is the kingdom of God.

Elder Boyd K. Packer has written of a remarkable experience regarding the keys of the kingdom, the directing powers by which families are sealed forever. "In 1976 an area general conference was held in Copenhagen, Denmark. Following the closing session, President Kimball expressed a desire to visit the Vor Frue Church, where the Thorvaldsen statues of the Christus and of the Twelve Apostles stand. He had visited this some years before. Others of us had also seen it but some had not, and he felt we should all go there.

"The church was closed for renovation, nevertheless arrangements were quickly made for us to be admitted for a few minutes. There were just a few of us.

"To the front of the church, behind the altar, stands the familiar statue of the Christus with his arms turned forward and somewhat outstretched, the hands showing the imprint of the nails, the wound in his side clearly visible. Along each side stand the statues of the Apostles, Peter at the front on the right side of the church, and the other Apostles in order. It is not a large building, and these beautiful statues make an impressive sight indeed.

"Most of the group were near the rear of the chapel, where the custodian, through an interpreter, was giving some explanation. I stood with President Kimball, Elder Rex Pinegar, and President Bentine, the stake president, before the statue of Peter. In his hand, depicted in marble, is a set of heavy keys. President Kimball pointed to them and explained what they symbolized. Then, in an act I shall never forget, he turned to President Bentine and with unaccustomed stern-ness pointed his finger at him and said with firm, impressive words, 'I want you to tell every Lutheran in Denmark that they do not hold the keys! I hold the keys! We hold the real keys and we use them every day.'

"This declaration and testimony from the prophet so affected me that I knew I would never forget it—the influence was powerfully spiritual and the impression was physical in its impact as well.

"We walked to the other end of the chapel where the rest of the group were standing. Pointing to the statues, President Kimball said to the kind custodian who was showing us the building, 'These are the dead Apostles. Here we have the living Apostles.' Pointing to me he said, 'Elder Packer is an Apostle.' He designated the others and said, 'Elder Monson and Elder Perry are Apostles, and I am an Apostle. We are the living Apostles. You read about seventies in the

New Testament, and here are living seventies, Brother Pinegar and Brother Hales'.

"The custodian, who to that time had shown no particular emotion, suddenly was in tears.

"As we left that little chapel where those impressive sculptures stand, I felt I had taken part in an experience of a lifetime" (*Holy Temple,* 83–84).

Ours is the day of restitution. Into the ocean of our dispensation flow the rivers and streams of dispensations past. It is necessary in our day and in a time yet future "that a whole and complete and perfect union, and welding together of dispensations, and keys, and powers, and glories should take place, and be revealed from the days of Adam even to the present time. And not only this, but those things which never have been revealed from the foundation of the world, but have been kept hid from the wise and prudent, shall be revealed unto babes and sucklings in this, the dispensation of the fulness of times" (D&C 128:18; compare 112:30–31). The keys of the kingdom of God—restored by such heavenly messengers as John the Baptist, Peter, James,

John, Moses, Elias, Elijah, Michael, Raphael, and divers angels (see D&C 128:20–21)—are here on earth to bless humanity. As the capstone to the blessings of the gospel, the powers restored by Elias and Elijah enable us to organize and seal family units for time and all eternity and to make of earth a heaven and of man a god.

# POWER IN THE COVENANT

There is power, consummate power, in the new and everlasting covenant. That power transcends our finite capacity to fully understand an infinite God's eternal plan to save all of those who will be saved. We know so little. In a world that presses for fairness, we too often close our eyes to the tender mercies of a loving Savior. The Master demonstrates his infinite mercy, for example, by refusing to condemn those who were ignorant of the gospel message and its requirements (see 2 Nephi 9:25–26; Mosiah 3:11; Moroni 8:22; D&C 137:7–9), including little children who died before the age of accountability (see Mosiah 3:16; 15:25; Moroni 8:8–12, 22; D&C 29:46–47; 74:7; 137:10). He offers the sublime gift—eternal life—to those laborers who join the work in the vineyard in the eleventh hour, the same gift he offers to those who have labored the entire day (see Matthew 20:1–16).

## Expanding Our Vision and Our Hope

The Prophet Joseph Smith called upon us to repent of littleness of soul and broaden our horizons. "It is the constitutional disposition of mankind to set up stakes and set bounds to the works and ways of the Almighty." And he warned: "I say to all those who are disposed to set up stakes for the Almighty, You will come short of the glory of God" (Smith, *Teachings of the Prophet Joseph Smith,* 320, 321). He also said: "Our heavenly Father is more liberal in His views, and boundless in His mercies and blessings, than we are ready to believe or receive." He continued: "The Lord Almighty has . . . so firmly established the dispensation of the fullness of the priesthood in the last days, that all the powers of earth and hell can never prevail against it" (Smith, *Teachings of the Prophet Joseph Smith,* 257, 258).

In speaking at the funeral for Judge Elias Higbee on 13 August 1843, the Prophet stated: "That which hath been hid from before the foundation of the world is revealed to babes and sucklings in the last days. The world is reserved unto burning in the last days. He shall send Elijah the prophet, and he shall reveal the covenants of the fathers in relation to the children, and the covenants of the children in relation to the fathers." He referred to the four angels of Revelation 7, described in modern revelation as "four angels sent forth from God, to whom is given power over the four parts of the earth, to save life and to destroy; these are they who have the everlasting gospel to commit to every nation, kindred, tongue, and people; having power to shut up the heavens, *to seal up unto life*, or to cast down to the regions of darkness" (D&C 77:8; emphasis added). The Prophet then declared: "Four destroying angels holding power over the four quarters of the earth until the servants of God are sealed in their foreheads, which signifies sealing the blessing upon their heads, meaning the everlasting covenant, thereby making their calling and election sure. *When a seal is put upon the father and mother, it secures their posterity, so that they cannot be lost, but will be saved by virtue of the covenant of their father and mother*" (Smith, *Teachings of the Prophet Joseph Smith*, 320–21; emphasis added).

Howard and Martha Coray recorded that same sermon as follows: "God shall send unto them Elijah the prophet and he shall reveal unto them the covenants of the fathers with relation to the children and the covenants of the children in relation to the Fathers that they may have the privilege of entering into the same in order to effect their mutual salvation" (Smith, *Words of Joseph Smith*, 240; punctuation and spelling standardized). Franklin D. Richards recorded the Prophet's words as follows: "Judge Higbee would say that covenants either there or here must be made in view of eternity. *The covenant sealed on the foreheads of the parents secured the children from falling* [and] that they shall all sit upon thrones as one with the godhead, joint heirs of God with Jesus Christ" (Smith, *Words of Joseph Smith*, 241; emphasis added and punctuation and spelling standardized).

What does this mean? To what degree can righteous parents, fathers and mothers who have entered into and kept sacred covenants, affect and effect the salvation of their posterity? President Brigham Young taught: "Let the father and mother, who are members of this Church and kingdom, take a righteous course, and strive with all their might never to do a wrong, but to do good all their lives; if they have one child or one hundred children, if they conduct themselves towards them as they should, binding them to the Lord by their faith and prayers, I care not where those children go, they are bound up to their parents by an everlasting tie, *and no power on earth or hell can separate them from their parents in eternity;* they will return again to the fountain from whence they sprang" (in *Journal of Discourses*, 11:215; emphasis added). We think of the sufferings and pleadings of Alma the Elder and his wife and remember the words of the angel to the wandering son: "Behold, the Lord hath heard the prayers of his people, and also the prayers of his servant, Alma, who is thy father; for he has prayed with much faith concerning thee that thou mightest be brought to the knowledge of the truth; therefore, for this purpose have I come to convince thee of the power and authority of God, that the prayers of his servants might be answered according to their faith" (Mosiah 27:14).

William Clayton's account of the Prophet Joseph's funeral address contains the following:

"When speaking of the passage 'I will send Elijah the prophet etc.,' he said it should read: 'And he shall turn the hearts of the children to the covenant made with their fathers'" (Smith, *Words of Joseph Smith*, 241–42; punctuation standardized). We believe that those who are faithful in their first estate come to the earth with certain predispositions to receive and embrace the truth. The Prophet himself declared that those of the house of Israel who come into the Church do so with quiet receptivity to the Spirit of the Lord and an openness to pure intelligence (see Smith, *Teachings of the Prophet Joseph Smith*, 149–50).

Similarly, we have no difficulty speaking of the "spirit of Elijah" reaching out, touching, directing, and impelling individuals to search out their dead and perform the saving ordinances. Why should we have difficulty believing that the power of the covenant will reach out, touch, redirect, and impel the wandering sheep? Could that power be indeed the same spirit of Elijah, the spirit that turns the hearts of the children to the covenant made with their fathers?

Elder Orson F. Whitney taught powerfully:

"You parents of the wilful and the wayward! Don't give them up. Don't cast them off. They are not utterly lost. The Shepherd will find his sheep. They were his before they were yours— long before he entrusted them to your care; and you cannot begin to love them as he loves them. They have but strayed in ignorance from the Path of Right, and God is merciful to ignorance. Only the fulness of knowledge brings the fulness of accountability. Our Heavenly Father is far more merciful, infinitely more charitable, than even the best of his servants, and the Everlasting Gospel is mightier in power to save than our narrow finite minds can comprehend.

"The Prophet Joseph Smith declared—and he never taught more comforting doctrine—that the eternal sealings of faithful parents and the divine promises made to them for valiant service in the Cause of Truth, would save not only themselves, *but likewise their posterity.* Though some of the sheep may wander, the eye of the Shepherd is upon them, and sooner or later they will feel the tentacles of Divine Providence reaching out after them and drawing them back to the fold. *Either in this life or in the life to come, they will return.* They will have to pay their debt to justice; they will suffer for their sins; and may tread a thorny path; but if it leads them at last, like the penitent Prodigal, to a loving and forgiving father's heart and home, the painful experience will not have been in vain. Pray for your careless and disobedient children; hold on to them with your faith. Hope on, trust on, till you see the salvation of God" (in Conference Report, Apr. 1929, 110; emphasis added).

In our own day, Elder Boyd K. Packer has provided a comforting context and reaffirmation for the promise to faithful parents: "It is a great challenge to raise a family in the darkening mists of our moral environment.

"We emphasize that the greatest work you will do will be within the walls of your home (see Harold B. Lee, in Conference Report, April 1973, p. 130), and that 'no other success can compensate for failure in the home' (see David O. McKay, in Conference Report, April 1935, p. 116).

"*The measure of our success as parents, however, will*

*not rest solely on how our children turn out.* That judgment would be just only if we could raise our families in a perfectly moral environment, and that now is not possible.

"It is not uncommon for responsible parents to lose one of their children, for a time, to influences over which they have no control. They agonize over rebellious sons and daughters. They are puzzled over why they are so helpless when they have tried so hard to do what they should. It is my conviction that those wicked influences one day will be overruled. . . .

"We cannot overemphasize the value of temple marriage, the binding ties of the sealing ordinance, and the standards of worthiness required of them. *When parents keep the covenants they have made at the altar of the temple, their children will be forever bound to them*" (in Conference Report, Apr. 1992, 94–95; emphasis added).

## Some Questions and Answers

This marvelous doctrine provides hope—a measure of peace and rest and assurance—to all who mourn over their wandering sheep. It is a revealed answer to some of the soul's longings for understanding. And yet there are additional questions that beckon for response. For example:

1. Will the power of the covenant coerce straying individuals into obedience?

We all know that even a merciful God will not violate an individual's moral agency, that he will force no man to heaven. Exaltation in the celestial kingdom is reserved for those who choose to go there, not those who are coerced or manipulated into appropriate behavior. We know that the laws of the everlasting covenant cannot violate the principles of justice or the canons of right and wrong. And yet there seems to be, in the sermons and writings of the prophets, the quiet but soul-satisfying message that the alms of the prayers of the righteous do come up into the ears of the Lord of Sabaoth; that righteous parents' loyalty to their covenants will not be overlooked; that no amount of suffering of the faithful in behalf of their posterity will be for naught; and that there is power, remarkable power, in the covenant to save those who will be saved. President Joseph Fielding Smith taught: "Those born under the covenant, throughout all eternity, are the children of their parents. Nothing except the unpardonable sin, or sin unto death, can break this tie. If children do not sin as John says [1 John 5:16–17], 'unto death,' the parents may still feel after them and eventually bring them back to them again" (*Doctrines of Salvation*, 2:90). As Elder Packer suggested, it may be that the power of evil in these last days is so oppressive that it chokes or restrains the proper exercise of agency. One day that will change.

2. Isn't the power or spirit of Elijah that which turns our hearts to our deceased loved ones?

The spirit of Elijah does indeed point our minds to those who went before, those who laid the foundation for what we now enjoy. Because Elijah came, we feel prompted and impelled to make available the sweet privileges of the gospel covenant to those who have not been so blessed. At the same time, Elijah's power and blessings pertain to the living. President Harold B. Lee explained that Elijah's mission "applies just as much on this side of the veil as it does on the other side of the veil. . . . So, the hearts of you fathers and mothers must be turned to your children right now, if you have the true spirit of Elijah, and not think that it applies merely to those who are beyond the veil" (Priesthood Genealogy Seminar, 1973).

3. Isn't it possible that one can stray so far as to forfeit blessings hereafter?

Yes, there are limits, not necessarily to God's mercy but the extent to which mercy can temper justice. In speaking of very serious sins, President Joseph F. Smith explained that a person can and will be forgiven if he repents: "The blood of Christ will make him free, and will wash him clean, though his sins be as scarlet; but all this will not return to him any loss sustained, nor place him on an equal footing with his neighbor who has kept the commandments of the better law. Nor will it place him in a position where he would have been, had he not committed wrong" (*Gospel Doctrine*, 374; see also Kimball, *Miracle of Forgiveness*, 310–11). President Joseph Fielding Smith declared that "children born under the covenant, who drift away, are still the children of their parents; and the parents have a claim upon them; and if the children have not sinned away all their rights, the parents may be able to bring them through repentance, into the celestial kingdom, but not to receive the exaltation" (*Doctrines of Salvation*, 2:91). That is why we teach that prevention is far, far better than redemption. Though we rejoice in the cleansing powers of the blood of our Redeemer, we must, as President Harold B. Lee observed, impress the members of the Church "with the awfulness of sin rather than to content ourselves with merely teaching the way of repentance" (*Decisions for Successful Living*, 88)

4. Doesn't the Prophet Joseph Smith's statement regarding the sealing of righteous parents seem to indicate that the parents' calling and election must be made sure?

Latter-day Saints who have received the ordinances of salvation—including the blessings of the temple endowment and eternal marriage—may press forward in the work of the Lord and with quiet dignity and patient maturity seek to be worthy of gaining the certain assurance of salvation before the end of their mortal lives. But should one not formally receive the more sure word of prophecy in this life, he has the scriptural promise that faithfully enduring to the end—keeping the covenants and commandments from baptism to the end of his life (see Mosiah 18:8–9)—eventuates in the promise of eternal life, whether that promise be received here or hereafter (see D&C 14:7; 53:7; see also 2 Nephi 31:20; Mosiah 5:15). "But blessed are they who are faithful and endure, whether in life or in death, for they shall inherit eternal life" (D&C 50:5).

Elder Bruce R. McConkie expressed the following sentiments at the funeral of Elder S. Dilworth Young: "If we die in the faith, that is the same thing as saying that our calling and election has been made sure and that we will go on to eternal reward hereafter. As far as faithful members of the Church are concerned, they have charted a course leading to eternal life. This life is the time that is appointed as a probation-ary estate for men to prepare to meet God, and as far as faithful people are concerned, if they are in line of their duty, if they are doing what they ought to do, although they may not have been perfect in this sphere, their probation is ended. Now there will be some probation for some other people hereafter. But for the faithful saints of God, now is the time and the day, and their probation is ended with their death" (funeral address, 13 July 1981).

5. Don't we believe that if a person rejects the gospel in this life that person will reject it in the world to come? Isn't it true that if one wanders from the fold here one is not likely to return hereafter?

Many years ago while working as a coun-selor, I met with a single mother who was strug-gling to rear three teenagers. She came in one afternoon particularly pensive. She said, "I have a big decision to make." She reminded me that her husband had been killed in an automobile accident exactly one year ago. "What's the problem?" I asked. "I need to decide whether to do his temple work," she responded. "Why is that even a problem for you? Didn't you love him?" "Yes," she said. "I adored him. He was a remarkable human being—a terrific father, a loving husband, a scouter in the community, a Little League baseball coach, an all-around great guy." She paused a moment and then added: "But he was not a member of the Church. He was very supportive of me and the children, was a moral and upright man, didn't smoke or drink, but he never took the restored gospel very seriously."

I asked again: "Well, what's the problem? Why don't you do his work?" She replied that one of her teachers had discouraged her from doing so. His words went something like this: "Look, he didn't accept the gospel here, and so he won't accept it hereafter. To go to the temple in his behalf would be a total waste of time." I was stunned but attempted to hold my composure, especially because the teacher she quoted was well known in the community and his word was highly regarded. She asked what I thought. I said: "Oh, I'd probably take a slightly different approach." "What's that?" "I would go to the temple this afternoon if I could," I said. "What do you mean?" she asked. I then explained that we are simply not in a position to judge, to know what's in a person's heart— what someone else feels, believes, knows. We do not really understand what constitutes a valid opportunity to hear the gospel, when the witness of the Spirit has been felt, or whether the message of the Restoration was even presented in a manner that was intelligible or truly inspirational. She had the work done a short time later.

Amulek did teach that the same spirit or disposition we have in this life will be with us in the world to come (see Alma 34:31–35), and the principle is true enough. Continuing in a habitually evil course makes it awfully difficult to change. But is it impossible? We must never deny another person the opportunity to change. People change here. Why can they not change hereafter? President Joseph F. Smith beheld in his vision of the postmortal spirit world how "the chosen messengers went forth to declare the acceptable day of the Lord and proclaim liberty to the captives who were bound, even unto all who would repent of their sins and receive the gospel." Now note this interesting verse: "Thus was the gospel preached to those who had died in their sins, without a knowledge of the truth, or in transgression, having rejected the prophets" (D&C 138:31–32). This same principle is echoed in the words of President Wilford Woodruff: "I tell you when the prophets and apostles go to preach to those who are shut up in prison, thousands of them will there embrace the Gospel. They know more in that world than they do here" (cited in Boyd K. Packer, *Holy Temple*, 206).

So many things can weigh upon the mind and heart of an individual: pressures and challenges and crosses that only God can see and comprehend. Why does a person reject the gospel? Why does a child wander? Can we see the whole picture? Are we in a position to pass appropriate judgment and close the doors to future recovery and reconciliation? I have a conviction that when a person passes through the veil of death, all those impediments and challenges and crosses that were beyond his or her power to control—abuse, neglect, immoral environment, weighty traditions, etc.—will be torn away like a film. Then perhaps that person shall, as President Woodruff suggested, see and feel things he or she could not see and feel before.

6. Don't these kinds of teachings motivate some young people to neglect their duty and "sow their wild oats"?

I suppose there will always be those who choose to take license in gospel liberty or who despise the saving grace of our Lord by knowingly violating the laws of God. There is always that risk. There is, however, what I perceive to be a greater risk—that well-meaning, hardworking, and diligent mothers and fathers with straying children may draw false conclusions about themselves and maybe even throw in the towel in despair. To such persons, the prophetic word concerning the consummate power of the covenant is manna to the soul, living water to parched lips. It may also be the case that such doctrine is often more effectively delivered and applied in more intimate settings. Bruce Hafen has written: "I was surprised on one occasion to hear a senior General Authority tell me something in a private conversation that allowed for greater flexibility on a particular issue than I had expected to hear. I told him how valuable I thought it would be if more members of the Church could hear his counsel, because what is said across the desk can so nicely clarify what is said over the pulpit. He replied that *private* counsel can be adapted to the attitudes and understanding of the person being counseled. If that same counsel were given publicly to an audience that included individuals of insufficient background or commitment, it might appear to give license to those whose needs require not more flexibility, but less" (*Broken Heart*, 4–5).

7. Is all of this really fair to those parents who have been successful in rearing their family or to

those children who have kept themselves from serious sin?

Stated bluntly, all of us are guilty of sin. All of us are in need of pardoning mercy. All of us fall short of the divine standard. During a long day of debate with his opponents, Jesus delivered the following parable: "A certain man had two sons; and he came to the first, and said, Son, go work to day in my vineyard. He [the son] answered and said, I will not: but afterward he repented, and went. And he came to the second, and said likewise. And he [the second son] answered and said, I go, sir: and went not. Whether of them twain did the will of his father?" (Matthew 21:28-31.) One "may wonder why this story does not include a third son who said, 'I will,' and kept his word. Perhaps it is because this story characterizes humanity, and we all fall short (Romans 3:23). Thus Jesus could describe only two kinds of religious people: those who pretend to be obedient but are actually rebels, and those who begin as rebels but repent" (MacArthur, *Gospel According to Jesus*, 167).

Obviously there are all types and varieties of

sin, and some are certainly more serious than others. At the same time, there should be no doubt in any of our hearts that each one of us receives far more of the goodness and grace of heaven than is just. On one occasion I was talking with a colleague about life here and the kinds of rewards that can come to us hereafter. I made some rather flippant comment to this effect: "I just want to get what I deserve." I was startled but instructed by my friend's response: "You had better pray to God that you don't get what you deserve!" Every one of us is and will forevermore be eternal debtors. Indeed, as King Benjamin taught, if we "should serve him who has created you from the beginning, and is preserving you from day to day, by lending you breath, that ye may live and move and do according to your own will, and even supporting you from one moment to another—I say, if ye should serve him with all your whole souls yet ye would be unprofitable servants" (Mosiah 2:21).

Inasmuch as each of us is a recipient of unending and unmerited grace, how can we, in the spirit of Christian charity—or in the attitude of sane discourse—speak of the Lord's pardoning mercy toward wayward children as unfair? Of course it's unfair! It's all unfair! That a pure and innocent man should suffer and agonize over others' transgressions is not fair. That he who had never taken a backward step should tread the winepress alone, "even the winepress of the fierceness of the wrath of Almighty God" (D&C 76:107; 88:106) and thereby descend below all things (see D&C 88:6), is not fair. That the lowly Nazarene should be subjected to the ignominy and unspeakable torture of crucifixion is patently not fair. But the plan of the Father is not a plan of fairness, at least as we judge fairness from our limited perspective; it is a plan of mercy. The Father and the Son love us in ways that we cannot comprehend. They will do all that is within the bounds of propriety to save as many of the posterity of Adam and Eve as will be saved. President J. Reuben Clark Jr. spoke of the goodness of our God: "I feel that [the Lord] will give that punishment which is the very least that our transgression will justify. . . . I believe that when it comes to making the rewards for our good conduct, he will give the maximum that is possible to give" ("As Ye Sow . . . ," 7–8; see also Clark, *Behold the Lamb of God*, 98).

There is power in righteousness, power that activates God's covenant with his people, power that binds and seals here and hereafter, power that links the children of Abraham, the children of the covenant, in love and unity. Righteous parents thereby affect generations to come. "Ye are the children of the prophets," the risen Lord declared to the Nephites; "and ye are of the house of Israel; and ye are of the covenant which the Father made with your fathers, saying unto Abraham: And in thy seed shall all the kindreds of the earth be blessed. The Father having raised me up unto you first, and sent me to bless you in turning away every one of you from his iniquities; and this because ye are the children of the covenant" (3 Nephi 20:25–26).

The pull of the covenant toward righteousness may come from both sides of the veil. The counsel of Elisha the prophet is still timely: "Fear not: for they that be with us are more than they that be with them" (2 Kings 6:16). My friend and colleague Joseph McConkie told me that his grandfather, Oscar McConkie Sr., said to the family just before his death: "I am going to die. When I die, I shall not cease to love you. I shall not cease to pray for you. I shall not cease to labor in your behalf." President Joseph F. Smith, in a conference address in April 1916 entitled "In the Presence of the Divine," made the following impressive and instructive remarks:

"Sometimes the Lord expands our vision from this point of view and this side of the veil, so that we feel and seem to realize that we can look beyond the thin veil which separates us from that other sphere. If we can see, by the enlightening influence of the Spirit of God and through the words that have been spoken by the holy prophets of God, beyond the veil that separates us from the spirit world, surely those who have passed beyond, can see more clearly through the veil back here to us than it is possible for us to see to them from our sphere of action. I believe we move and have our being in

the presence of heavenly messengers and of
heavenly beings. We are not separate from them.
We begin to realize, more and more fully, as we
become acquainted with the principles of the
gospel, as they have been revealed anew in this
dispensation, that we are closely related to our
kindred, to our ancestors, to our friends and
associates and co-laborers who have preceded
us into the spirit world. We can not forget them;
we do not cease to love them; we always hold
them in our hearts, in memory. . . . How much
more certain it is and reasonable and consistent
to believe that those who have been faithful,
who have gone beyond and are still engaged in
the work for the salvation of the souls of men,
. . . can see us better than we can see them; that
they know us better than we know them. They
have advanced; we are advancing; we are grow-
ing as they have grown; we are reaching the
goal that they have attained unto; and therefore,
I claim that we live in their presence, they see us,
they are solicitous for our welfare, they love us
now more than ever. For now they see the dan-
gers that beset us; they can comprehend, better

than ever before, the weaknesses that are liable
to mislead us into dark and forbidden paths.
They see the temptations and the evils that beset
us in life and the proneness of mortal beings to
yield to temptation and to wrong doing; hence
their solicitude for us, and their love for us, and
their desire for our well being, must be greater
than that which we feel for ourselves" (in Clark,
*Messages of the First Presidency*, 5:6–7).

"Rewards for obedience to the commandments," Elder Russell M. Nelson taught, "are
almost beyond mortal comprehension. Here,
children of the covenant become a strain of sin-
resistant souls. And hereafter, . . . children of the
covenant, and 'each generation [will] be linked
to the one which went on before . . . [in] the
divine family of God' [Joseph Fielding Smith, in
Conference Report, Apr. 1965, 10]. Great comfort
comes from the knowledge that our loved ones
are secured to us through the covenants" (in
Conference Report, Apr. 1995, 33–43).

# EPILOGUE

T hen drew near unto [Jesus] all the publicans and sinners for to hear him. And the Pharisees and scribes murmured, saying, This man receiveth sinners, and eateth with them." The Master then delivered three parables of lost things—a lost sheep, a lost coin, and a lost son. The Prophet Joseph Smith taught us how to interpret parables. "I enquire, what was the question which drew out the answer, or caused Jesus to utter the parable. . . . To ascertain its meaning, we must dig up the root and ascertain what it was that drew the saying out of Jesus" (Smith, *Teachings of the Prophet Joseph Smith,* 276–77). Although we may appropriately seek after and supply many applications to a parable, there is only one interpretation. The three parables of lost things in Luke 15 are parables of chastisement. Jesus is there condemning the self-righteousness of those who cannot discern the pride in their own supposed goodness.

## The First Parable

"And he spake this parable unto them, saying, What man of you, having an hundred sheep, if he lose one of them, doth not leave the ninety and nine in the wilderness, and go after that which is lost, until he find it? And when he hath found it, he layeth it on his shoulders, rejoicing. And when he cometh home, he calleth together his friends and neighbours, saying unto them, Rejoice with me; for I have found my sheep which was lost. I say unto you, that likewise joy shall be in heaven over one sinner that repenteth, more than over ninety and nine just persons, which need no repentance" (Luke 15:3–7).

Here is a case of a prized possession that wanders off, on its own, in search of food. We suppose not neglect on the part of the shepherd but rather distraction and inattention on the part of the foolish sheep. The one sheep is precious, worthy of extra effort, worthy of the risk of leaving the ninety and nine for a brief season. Besides, the ninety and nine sheep are just as lost in their own way.

The Prophet explained: "The hundred sheep represent one hundred Sadducees and Pharisees, as though Jesus had said, 'If you Sadducees and Pharisees are in the sheepfold, I have no mission for you; I am sent to look up sheep that are lost; and when I have found them, I will back them up and make joy in heaven.' This represents hunting after a few individuals, or one poor publican, which the Pharisees and Sadducees despised" (Smith, *Teachings of the Prophet Joseph Smith*, 277).

Indeed, when the Good Shepherd has found one that is lost, he lifts and lightens the burdens of the wanderer, takes the weight of sin upon his back, and leads the sheep back to safety within the household of faith. In like manner, those of us who are disciples of Christ are called as undershepherds, as apprentices to the merciful and forgiving One. We are once again reminded of the words of the Prophet Joseph on this matter. "The nearer we get to our heavenly Father, the more we are disposed to look with compassion on perishing souls; we feel that we want to take them upon our shoulders, and cast their sins behind our backs" (Smith, *Teachings of the Prophet Joseph Smith*, 241).

## The Second Parable

"Either what woman having ten pieces of silver, if she lose one piece, doth not light a candle, and sweep the house, and seek diligently till she find it? And when she hath found it, she calleth her friends and her neighbours together, saying, Rejoice with me; for I have found the piece which I had lost. Likewise, I say unto you, there is joy in the presence of the angels of God over one sinner that repenteth" (Luke 15:8–10).

In this second parable, a precious item is lost because of the neglect of the owner. Again, this is a parable of chastisement, an accusation against those who see themselves as perpetually faithful. The Prophet stated: "There is joy in the presence of the angels of God over one sinner that repenteth, more than over ninety-and-nine just persons that are so righteous; they [the prideful ones] will be damned anyhow; you cannot save them" (Smith, *Teachings of the Prophet Joseph Smith*, 277–78).

In the parable, the woman's heart seems to be right, her motives pure, her desire to retrieve the lost item genuine. It certainly isn't something she planned to do; unfortunately, it was mis-placed. In the same way, a brother or sister may be lost through our neglect: perhaps we weren't regular or consistent in our visits; perhaps we weren't as loving and welcoming as we might have been when he or she came to church; per-haps we weren't as willing to forgive and forget as we should have been. Perhaps the man or woman was too eager to be hurt, too quick to take offense, too open to bruising by an ecclesi-astical elbow. Whatever the cause, the under-shepherds search and watch and reach out in earnest anticipation that the wandering one may be found. And the angels— including loved ones on both sides of the veil—exult in the reunion.

## The Third Parable

The final parable of lost things is the most beloved of the three—the parable of the prodi-gal son. This parable distills the essence of the Christian message: that men and women who wander from the strait and narrow path may through sincere repentance be welcomed back by the Father into the fold of the royal family. It is a story that might be told of so many of us, a tale of one who left the comfort and security of a righteous home and wandered for a season into forbidden territory. "And when he had spent all, there arose a mighty famine in that land; and he began to be in want" (Luke 15:14). Indeed, once wanderers hit bottom, particularly those who have been taught better and have lived for a time in the light, it is fairly common for them to "come to themselves." They realize what they once had; they recognize the famine for the word of truth in their own lives in the present emptiness of their souls; deep within their hearts they begin to long for the sweet peace they once knew. Those who view themselves "in their own carnal state, even less than the dust of the earth" (Mosiah 4:2) feel the need to confess their sins and acknowledge their spiritual bankruptcy before God.

As the prodigal begins the long and arduous return home, while he or she is yet a great way off, the parents, loved ones, or church leaders— no doubt looking down the road regularly and hoping and praying incessantly for a miracle—see signs of progress, be they ever so slight. The arms of family and friends are opened wider, outpourings of compassion and pure love take place, and all rejoice. All, that is, except those who feel in some way cheated or slighted because the returning one is given a robe, a ring, and a fatted calf. "Lo, these many years do I serve thee," the faithful son responds to the joyful father, "neither transgressed I at any time thy commandment: and yet thou never gavest me a kid, that I might make merry with my friends: but as soon as this thy son was come, which hath devoured thy living with harlots, thou hast killed for him the fatted calf" (Luke 15:29–30). In fact, one application of the parable might be a warning against wandering and the price of sin. And, as we have already noted, prevention is far better than redemption.

Nevertheless, for the Eternal Father to say to one of us "all that I have is thine" in no way precludes any of the rest of us from inheriting and receiving the same reward of eternal life.

There is no ceiling on the number of saved beings. If in fact the elder of the sons was true and faithful, we rejoice with him and his parents. We in no way detract from his glory or his eternal attainment by allowing another who was less faithful for a time to repent and come back. Whether we stray out of ignorance (like the lost sheep), out of neglect (like the lost coin), or knowingly (like the prodigal son), the Almighty, who is a concerned Parent as well as our God, stands ready and willing to receive us back and reinstate us in the royal family. "It was meet that we should make merry, and be glad: for this thy brother was dead, and is alive again; and was lost, and is found" (Luke 15:32).

This supernal message is echoed in all scripture. If there is a central message that comes through the allegory of Zenos in the Book of Mormon, it is that Israel's God simply will not let Israel go. Jacob comments prophetically on that lengthy allegory: "And how merciful is our God unto us, for he remembereth the house of Israel, both roots and branches; and he stretches forth his hands unto them all the day long. . . .

Wherefore, my beloved brethren, I beseech of you in words of soberness that ye would repent, and come with full purpose of heart, and cleave unto God as he cleaveth unto you" (Jacob 6:4–5). What is true of a nation is equally true of individuals. Few of us in this life will through our sins place ourselves beyond the pale of saving grace.

God cherishes each one of us, not simply because we are his children, which is itself a powerful incentive for him to save as many as possible, but also because our Lord and Savior has paid an infinite price for us. We are a peculiar, meaning a *purchased,* people. We have been redeemed, not through an exchange of corruptible things but instead "with the precious blood of Christ, as of a lamb without blemish and without spot" (1 Peter 1:18–19). Something so costly cannot be ignored or treated lightly. "Remember the worth of souls is great in the sight of God; for, behold, the Lord your Redeemer suffered death in the flesh; wherefore he suffered the pain of all men, that all men might repent and come unto him. And he hath risen again from the dead, that he might bring all men unto him, on conditions of repentance. And how great is his joy in the soul that repenteth! Wherefore, you are called to cry repentance unto this people. And if it so be that you should labor all your days in crying repentance unto this people, and bring, save it be one soul unto me, how great shall be your joy with him in the kingdom of my Father! And now, if your joy will be great with one soul that you have brought unto me into the kingdom of my Father, how great will be your joy if you should bring many souls unto me!" (D&C 18:10–16).

## A Concluding Testimony

Let us ponder on what we have discussed relative to the power of the gospel covenant to secure and bind families.

The family is the most important unit in time and in eternity. No work, no service, no outside agency or interests can supersede the family in eternal significance. Even though the challenges of this life—including the demands for acclaim, prestige, acquisition of this world's goods—may pull tenaciously and constantly at us, some things simply matter more than others.

Few families in this life are spared the pain of wandering children or other loved ones. There are no greater feelings of helplessness than those associated with witnessing a loved one stray from the path of truth, follow alternate voices, or forsake the covenant life. We anguish, we stew, we pray, and we long for a miracle. Sometimes anguishing parents live to see their children return in this life, live to see the miracle for which they had pleaded for so long. And sometimes parents do not live to see the child return, but they do experience another kind of miracle—the soothing peace of the Prince of Peace, who provides strength, comfort, and divine perspective.

We are a people of covenant. Those who proved faithful in their first estate come to earth through a designated lineage and are heirs of the gospel covenant. Theirs is a predisposition to recognize truth, receive truth, and cleave unto truth.

The gospel of Jesus Christ is the new and

everlasting covenant. The power to enter into covenant, as well as to seal and ratify those covenants eternally—the keys of the kingdom of God—have been restored in our day by heavenly messengers. These blessings are available to each of us through the covenants and ordinances of the holy temple.

The Holy One of Israel, who is the Mediator of the covenant, has promised that when a seal is placed upon a father and mother—a seal that comes through faithfulness to their eternal covenants—their children will be bound to them forever. Even if the children stray, the tentacles of the everlasting covenant will feel after them and they shall, either here or hereafter, return to the fold. We do not fully understand all of the implications of this marvelous promise, but we trust in the ransoming and redeeming power of our Lord who is also our Savior.

"God has fulfilled his promises to us," President Lorenzo Snow explained, "and our prospects are grand and glorious. Yes, in the next life we will have our wives, and our sons and daughters. If we do not get them all at once, we will have them some time, for every knee shall bow and every tongue shall confess that Jesus is the Christ. You that are mourning about your children straying away will have your sons and your daughters. If you succeed in passing through these trials and afflictions and receive a resurrection, you will, by the power of the Priesthood, work and labor, as the Son of God has, until you get all your sons and daughters in the path of exaltation and glory. This is just as sure as that the sun rose this morning over yonder mountains. Therefore, mourn not because all your sons and daughters do not follow in the path that you have marked out to them, or give heed to your counsels. *Inasmuch as we succeed in securing eternal glory, and stand as saviors, and as kings and priests to our God, we will save our posterity. . . . God* will have His own way in His own time, and He will accomplish His purposes in the salvation of His sons and daughters. . . . God bless you, brethren and sisters. *Do not be discouraged* is the word I wish to pass to you; but remember that righteousness and joy in the Holy Ghost is what you and I have the privilege of possessing at all times" (address delivered 6 Oct. 1893; in Stuy, *Collected Discourses*, 3:364–65; emphasis added).

Several years ago my wife and I were struggling with how best to build faith in all of our children and how to entice wandering souls back into Church activity. A caring colleague, sensing the weight of my burdens, happened into my office one day and asked, "Do you think our heavenly parents wander through the heavens in morose agony over their straying children?" Startled, I thought for a moment and said, "No, I don't think so. I know they feel pain, but I honestly can't picture them living in eternal misery." My friend responded, "Ask yourself why they do not do so, and it will make a difference in your life." I didn't get much work done the rest of the day, because I spent many hours pondering the question. When I arrived home that evening, I asked Shauna to sit down and reflect on the same question. She answered as I had, and then the two of us set about a prayerful quest for the next several days to understand how our Eternal Father and Mother deal with their pain.

In time it began to dawn on us that the Lord knows the end from the beginning and that, as Joseph the Prophet declared, all things—past, present, and future—are and were with him "one eternal 'now'" (Smith, *Teachings of the Prophet Joseph Smith*, 220). Perspective. PERSPECTIVE. That was the answer. God deals with pain through and by virtue of his infinite and perfect perspective. He not only knows what we have done and what we are doing, but he also knows what we will do in the future. If, as the prophets have taught, many who are heirs to the blessings of the covenant made with Abraham, Isaac, and Jacob will either in time or in eternity be reconciled to the covenant family, then all we need to do for the time being is to seek through fasting and prayer for a portion of our God's perspective—his omniloving patience, his long-suffering, his ever-open arms, and a glimpse of the big picture. Such a perspective will not only serve us well here, in the midst of our sufferings, but it will empower our souls and fashion us into the image of our Master, who is the personification and embodiment of charity, or the pure love of Christ (see Moroni 7:45–48).

Because we are mortal, because we are human, because we cannot see the end from the beginning, when a child wanders we fret and ache and sometimes despair. But there is hope smiling brightly before us, hope that springs from the elevated perspective provided by the power of the gospel covenant. President Gordon B. Hinckley, in addressing the Saints in Great Britain, said: "May you be blessed, each of you. May there be love and peace and gladness in your homes. I leave my blessing upon you. May there be food on your table, clothing on your backs, shelter over your heads and a sense of security and peace and love among your children, precious children every one of them, even those who may have strayed. I hope you don't lose patience with them; I hope you go on praying for them, and I don't hesitate to promise that if you do so, the Lord will touch their hearts and bring them back to you with love and respect and appreciation" (*Church News*, 2 Sept. 1995, 4).

"There is never a time," the Prophet Joseph

Smith observed, "when the spirit is too old to approach God. All are within the reach of pardoning mercy, who have not committed the unpardonable sin" (Smith, *Teachings of the Prophet Joseph Smith*, 191). And so we pray, we fast, we plead, and we implore. And, perhaps most important, we love those who wander, and we never, never give up hope. I testify that there is a God in heaven who is our Eternal Father and that he lives in the family unit; that our Heavenly Father knows us one and all by name and knows perfectly our sorrows and our soul's deepest longings; that Jesus, as the Good Shepherd, will go in search of the lost ones; that the gospel covenant is as broad and deep and penetrating as eternity; and that there are righteous forces at work that are beyond our capacity to perceive or comprehend. I know, with all my heart, that "the effectual fervent prayer of a righteous man [or woman] availeth much" (James 5:16), and that both in time and in eternity our God shall wipe away all tears (see Isaiah 25:8; Revelation 7:17; 21:4).

We trust in the power of Christ, the Mediator

of the covenant, to forgive, to repair, to renew, and to rekindle the gospel light within the hearts of those who stray for a season. And we take comfort in the Master's promise: "Be faithful and diligent in keeping the commandments of God, and I will encircle thee in the arms of my love" (D&C 6:20).

# BIBLIOGRAPHY

Ballard, Melvin J. *Melvin J. Ballard: Crusader for Righteousness.* Salt Lake City: Bookcraft, 1966.

Ballard, M. Russell. In Conference Report, Oct. 1992, 41–45.

Benson, Ezra Taft. "What I Hope You Will Teach Your Children about the Temple." *Ensign*, Aug. 1985, 6–10.

Clark, James R., comp. *Messages of the First Presidency of The Church of Jesus Christ of Latter-day Saints.* 6 vols. Salt Lake City: Bookcraft, 1965–75.

Clark, J. Reuben, Jr. "As Ye Sow    " Address delivered at Brigham Young University, 3 May 1955

——. *Behold the Lamb of God.* Salt Lake City: Deseret Book, 1991.

Dunn, Loren C. In Conference Report, Apr. 1981, 32–36.

Faust, James E. In Conference Report, Apr. 1993, 44–47.

Hafen, Bruce C. *The Broken Heart.* Salt Lake City: Deseret Book, 1989.

Hinckley, Gordon B. In Conference Report, Apr. 1991, 93–98.

——. "Discourse." *Church News*, 2 Sept. 1995, 4.

Holland, Jeffrey R., and Patricia T. Holland. *On Earth As It Is in Heaven.* Salt Lake City: Deseret Book, 1989.

Kimball, Spencer W. *The Miracle of Forgiveness.* Salt Lake City: Bookcraft, 1969.

Lee, Harold B. *Decisions for Successful Living.* Salt Lake City: Deseret Book, 1973.

——. In Conference Report, Apr. 1973, 125–31.

——. In Conference Report, Oct. 1973, 3–10.

——. Priesthood Genealogy Seminar, 1973.

MacArthur, John F., Jr. *The Gospel According to Jesus.* Grand Rapids, Mich.: Academie Books, 1988.

McConkie, Bruce R. *A New Witness for the Articles of Faith.* Salt Lake City: Deseret Book, 1985.

——. Address at the funeral for S. Dilworth Young, 13 July 1981. Typescript.

——. "The Bible: A Sealed Book." In *The Eighth Annual Church Educational System Symposium on the New Testament.* Salt Lake City: The Church of Jesus Christ of Latter-day Saints, 1984.

——. *The Millennial Messiah: The Second Coming of the Son of Man.* Salt Lake City: Deseret Book, 1982.

——. *The Mortal Messiah: From Bethlehem to Calvary.* 4 vols. Salt Lake City: Deseret Book, 1979–81.

McKay, David O. In Conference Report, Apr. 1935, 110–16.

Millet, Robert L. *Within Reach.* Salt Lake City: Deseret Book, 1995.

Millet, Robert L., and Joseph Fielding McConkie. *The Life Beyond.* Salt Lake City: Bookcraft, 1986.

———. *Our Destiny: The Call and Election of the House of Israel.* Salt Lake City: Bookcraft, 1993.

Nelson, Russell M. In Conference Report, Apr. 1995, 111–16.

———. "Thanks for the Covenant." In *1988 89 Brigham Young University Devotional and Fireside Speeches.* Provo: Brigham Young University Publications, 1989.

Packer, Boyd K. *Problems in Teaching the Moral Standard.* Brigham Young University Speeches of the Year. Provo, 15 July 1958.

———. In Conference Report, Apr. 1987, 24–28.

———. In Conference Report, Apr. 1992, 91–95.

———. *Let Not Your Heart Be Troubled.* Salt Lake City: Bookcraft, 1991.

———. *That All May Be Edified.* Salt Lake City: Bookcraft, 1982.

———. *The Holy Temple.* Salt Lake City: Bookcraft, 1980.

Smith, Joseph. *Teachings of the Prophet Joseph Smith.* Sel. Joseph Fielding Smith. Salt Lake City: Deseret Book, 1976.

———. *The Words of Joseph Smith.* Comp. Andrew F. Ehat and Lyndon W. Cook. Provo: Brigham Young University Religious Studies Center, 1980.

Smith, Joseph F. *Gospel Doctrine.* Salt Lake City: Deseret Book, 1971.

Smith, Joseph Fielding. *Doctrines of Salvation.* 3 vols. Comp. Bruce R. McConkie. Salt Lake City: Bookcraft, 1954–56.

Snow, Lorenzo. *The Teachings of Lorenzo Snow.* Comp. Clyde J. Williams. Salt Lake City: Bookcraft, 1984.

Stuy, Brian H., comp. *Collected Discourses Delivered by*

President Wilford Woodruff, His Two Counselors, the Twelve Apostles, and Others. 5 vols. Burbank, Calif.: B. H. S. Publishing, 1987–92.

Top, Brent L. *The Life Before.* Salt Lake City: Bookcraft, 1988.

Whitney, Orson F. In Conference Report, Apr. 1929, 109–15.

# INDEX

*Index*

164